This book is dedicated to
Peter and Anth[o]
who had the foresight to have chil[dren with loving]
partners.

They have given their offspring the greatest gift of all,
the gift of love
and the confidence to face the world.

Thank you

Sharron

Clare

For five well adjusted and magnificent girls

Rachel

Rosie

Isobel

Keara

Rhianna

Contents:

Page Number:

Introduction	**1**
Personal information	13
Calendar	15
Housing issues and information	**19**
Inventory	36
Security	37
Police: Stop and Search	**39**
Bailiffs	41
C.C.J	44
Solicitors	**45**
Banking	**48**
Taxation and National Insurance	58
Insurance	60
D.I.Y	64
Health	78
Sex, facts and myths	**106**
General Problems	112
Hygiene	121
First aid	122
Cooking and food	**133**
Recipes	164
Your car	168
Your top 10 countries to visit	174
Passport	175
Royal Mail	177
Buying goods and Citizens Advice	180
Help lines and organisations	**183**
Political help	190
Clothing and laundry	192
Household tips	195
Understanding Religion	201
Employment issues	206
Making a Will	208
Games and puzzles	209

In The Beginning...

When I left home for the first time it was for me, for educational reasons. I was quite lucky I suppose. Off I went down the M6, car bursting with belongings, completely unaware of the trials and tribulations that were to come. Had someone told me there and then I am sure I would have turned round immediately and headed back, tail between legs, to the comfort and safety of home. Thankfully I carried on and learnt that first important lesson in how to cope 'on my own'. There were many things I wasn't expecting like the bills, meters, electric and gas and then the routine of driving around after work at 11pm just to find a parking space and of course then there's the neighbours. Noisy neighbours, smelly neighbours, I love ABBA neighbours, again I guess I was lucky compared to some. Sometimes I could have done with a helping hand, even with the most basic of things, I am embarrassed to admit.

This book has been written primarily to help you through those first few weeks away from home. Whether you are a student, leaving home because of family problems or just feel it is now the right time to make a move and need some independence, whatever your reasons you will need help and I hope you will find something here that will help you.

No matter what the circumstances the first few weeks are critical. You will ask yourself time and time again 'why did I do it?' and you will probably want to give in. If you feel you can simply not manage and it would be better to go back home then do so, however you will still crave that independent feeling and will still say to yourself "I have to do this sometime".

Hang on in there and I promise as each day passes life WILL get better and easier.

No matter who you are, at some point you will be lonely. The film star, businessman and even the life and soul of the party socialite feel alone and depressed at times, it is how you deal with it that matters. Sometimes you have to remind yourself: There is no-one that can help you more than you, no-one knows you like you and no-one feels exactly the same as you.

You have your own emotions and instincts and are more capable than you think. The human body, especially the mind, are capable of so much; you would be amazed how much you can achieve. To make these achievements it is important to forget completely what anyone else thinks of you, especially when they have a bad tongue and make you feel as if you are on the bottom of their shoe. Don't let these kinds of people knock you, deep down somewhere inside you know exactly what you want, just stay on the track to get it.

DETERMINATION IS THE KEY

The worst thing I am sure I can tell you now is that later in life you say:

'If only I had done that' OR I could have been.

There will always be those who laugh at what you want to achieve, those waiting for you to make mistakes and you WILL make mistakes because failure, as we are told so many times, is the only way to learn. It is annoying but true and believe me, it is the best way to learn. The list of those who failed constantly before making success is endless, but those who made this list should be proud for daring to follow their dreams and for using their god given talents to achieve those ultimate aims.

If you are going through hell, keep going.

 **Beethoven**, who was probably the greatest ever composer was told by his music teacher that he was a failure

Winston Churchill failed the sixth grade.

 **Thomas Edison's** teacher told him he was too stupid to learn

Louise M Alcott (little women) was told by an editor that she wouldn't write anything that anyone would like.

 **Enrico Caruso** (acknowledged by experts as the worlds greatest ever tenor) was told by his singing coach that he couldn't sing at all.

Abraham Lincoln entered the war as a captain and finished as a private.

 **F.W.Woolworth's** employer wouldn't let him serve customers because he didn't have enough sense.

A newspaper fired **Walt Disney** because he lacked 'ideas' and 'vision.'

 **Michael Jordon** was dropped from his high school basketball team went home locked the door and cried all day.

The Beatles in 1962 were turned down by Decca; they were told groups with guitars were on their way out.

 **Daniel Defoe** took his book Robinson Crusoe to twenty publishers before it was accepted.

The greatest rock and roller of all time **Elvis** was turned down by his high school glee club.

 The first agent to whom **J.K Rowling** sent 'Harry Potter and the Philosopher's Stone' rejected her in a little more than a day.
Her second agent Christopher Little, was turned down by 12 publishers before Bloomsbury a year later.

Neil Diamond was fired by his first five music publishers

 Probably the biggest failure and eventual successor was **Henry Ford**, who went broke five times.

 **Quaker oats** has been bankrupt three times, as well as three time loser **Pepsi cola** and believe it or not the same happened for **Wrigley's chewing gum.**

Birds eye frozen foods were lucky, they only went bust once.

These famous people kicked adversity into touch and so can you, as with Robert the Bruce and the spider.

Try, try and try again!

But surely one of the greatest turnarounds from adversity to triumph in history has to be the **Leaning Tower of Pisa**. Built in 1173 the tower has been plagued with structural problems since its design…hence its name.

However despite such adversity it has become one of the most visited tourist attractions in the world.

This is a great lesson for you…always try to turn a negative to your advantage.

It is such a crime to waste talent you are born with; you will always run into those critics calling your ideas silly or impossible. As you will gather I hate critics and knockers with a vengeance. Anyone can criticise or pour cold water on aspirations, go out and grab life with both hands and prove those knockers wrong.

In some ways I suppose it is important to encounter these people, if only to know what to look out for in the future. Other people however can give you valuable comments on how to better your idea, you can always listen to someone's opinion good or bad, at the end of the day you will know whether to follow their advice or not. Believe in yourself and be strong.

'Carpe Diem'
(Seize the day)

Success is so much sweeter when it is achieved in the face of adversity. Make a list of what you want to achieve and be happy when you get there, there is no time limit, you set this for yourself, however try not to leave your plans on the sideline when life suddenly takes over – which it will many times. The more effort and energy you put into your idea the more you will get from it in the end. The harder you work on your ideas or beliefs the luckier you will become. Along the way you can help yourself further by helping others, in any business and even in life itself you can never have too many friends or contacts.

This is not a blueprint or panacea but a series of articles covering a huge area of subjects to help you with your move and to ease you with settling into your new home. I hope that the chapters will help you to become confident in subjects unheard of, forgotten or simply not known.
It is very hard to do it on your own, if help is available then take it because it will be easier.

Never be afraid to ask for help.

Leaving home can give you the freedom and space you so desperately need but the extra responsibility can be extremely hard to adjust to. It's not always easy to find the right place to live and of course living on your own can be expensive.

The choices you have when you leave home will depend on your income eg, as a student there is sometimes help available for you to pay your rent, the same also applies for individuals with a low income, your local council may be able to help you.

It is important however to remember all the other costs such as:
- Gas, electricity, water, telephone and internet bills – you may even need to pay to get these services connected, so be aware of this.
- You will need extra money simply to eat and for travel expenses.
- You may also need furniture and other household items.

What to Do If you Fall Behind with Bills

Don't just do nothing!!! Contact your electricity/gas/water supplier, it's in their interest to help you pay the bills otherwise they'll be out of pocket! They might suggest that you pay smaller amounts over a period of time, but the sooner you contact them the less debt you will get into. Gas and electricity companies won't disconnect your home unless they have no choice however if you don't contact them, unless you are a pensioner or have one in your household, there is a chance they might disconnect yours. If you feel you need more help or advice about falling behind on the bills you can contact your local citizens' advice bureau.

It will be a big change and it is important to think every possibility through and make sure you're ready, not just financially but emotionally, it may be a big shock when you realise just how much cleaning, cooking and shopping there is to do.

Other things to think about:
- **-Will you live on your own or maybe share with a housemate?**
- **-Where will you live? Near to family and friends?**
- **-Do you need parking or be near to public transport?**
- **-Will you be entitled to any benefits/allowances?**
- **-Always look around a few properties before you make a decision.**

LIFE SAVERS

Follow these simple rules and it will all become so much easier

Remember the 5 P's:

No, not panic, panic, panic, panic, panic, but

Proper Planning Promotes Peak Performance…

ALWAYS pay bills the day they come in, this will give you more time if you do get into financial difficulties as most payments will have been made and you will have 3-4 weeks to catch up again.

KEEP receipts as they are your proof of payment, keep a box somewhere handy and you will soon get in the habit of putting all receipts in here.

LISTS are always helpful, as are reminders to those of us who are forgettable. Write a list of what needs to be done, highlight the points least liked or those you are most afraid to do.

…..Remember, if you go to bed with a problem it will still be there in the morning, your mind will have magnified it, if it's a big problem your night was probably filled with bad dreams and you will not be completely rested. To then tackle this problem will be just like trying to solve it yesterday. Try to solve problems on the day, even just to give yourself a good nights rest, once solved the problem is never as big as it once seemed and the relief you will feel will be most rewarding.

Never try to solve your problem with drink or drugs. This action will only ever make other people rich and send you spiralling down to where they will then tread upon you.
It may seem a good idea at times to indulge in this activity to forget your circumstances constantly at the forefront of your mind however the problem will therefore never be dealt with and the next day, or week, or even month in some cases, it's still haunting you, that small issue which is now huge and has probably taken over much of your life.

'Save a penny more than you spend'.

Do not take the advice of a Barrack room lawyer seek out the services of a professional solicitor or organisation.
If a solicitor gives you bad advice they can always be sued.

Procrastination is a sin. (Procrastinate – to delay/defer, put off to a future time).
Whatever your ideas or beliefs are, act on them now.

A journey of a thousand miles starts with a thousand steps.
Chairman Mao

Two of my favourite sayings that might help you in some way are:

-Nothing in the world can take the place of persistence,
Talent will not;
Nothing is more common than unsuccessful men with talent,
Genius will not;
Un-rewarded genius is almost a proverb,
Education will not;
The world is full of educated derelicts,
Persistence and determination alone are omnipotent.

-*If only the birds that sang the best, sang...*
**The forest would be a very quiet place.*

After you've left

Whatever you left home for you have probably left parents behind. Good, bad or indifferent they are the only ones you will ever have. If you have disappeared without telling anyone this can be traumatic and soul destroying for your family. Not knowing if you are dead or alive, well or ill means in many cases real torment. Always keep in touch just one call can make all the difference. You have no need to say where you are. Even if you ring just once a month  to say that you are all right it could make all the difference. One call means so much.

Not only does it affect those you have left behind to many lives have been destroyed by feelings of guilt. Your parents or members of your family could pass on or have a serious illness without you knowing. You would never forgive yourself and the consequences could affect the rest of your life.

Do it now –

Make someone happy!

If you are 16 or 17, you can leave home with parental consent. If you leave against their will, they can take action to get you home through the courts or by reporting you missing to the police. Even then, if you can show you are able to look after yourself and are safe, the police are unlikely to get involved. At 18 you can leave home without parental consent.

At this point I would like to make a special mention of group of people who probably feel that life has already dealt them a series of body blows, I refer of course to the people who have spent all or part of their lives in care, either in care homes or fostered out to various households.

In a lot of cases they may feel unloved or unwanted but in some ways you are in a better position than most because you have already experienced some of the hardships of life.
This is in no way a criticism whatsoever of the care system the majority of people who look after young people do a magnificent job but doesn't always compare to the affection that your own family could give.

It is important at this point in your life to think of the future rather than the past, it is more important to concentrate on where you are going than where you came from.

You think you have to prove your existence but life has probably made you a much stronger person than your average teenager and you have got to treat that as a plus as opposed to a negative.

We are all born equal and go out as equals,
But sometimes fate gets in the way.

I want you to make this your motto and say this everyday:

"If I want it to be, it's up to me."

It's not important where you came from it's the direction you're going in and where you end up.

I believe as Barnardo's do
"that the lives of all children and young people should be free from poverty, abuse and discrimination."

Personal Information

Name:	………………………………………..
Address:	………………………………………..
	…………………………………………..
	…………………………………………..
	…………………………………………..
Telephone Number:	………………………………..
Mobile Number:	………………………………..
E-Mail:	……………………………………….
Passport Number:	………………………………..
National Insurance Number:	……………………………….
Driving Licence Number:	………………………………..

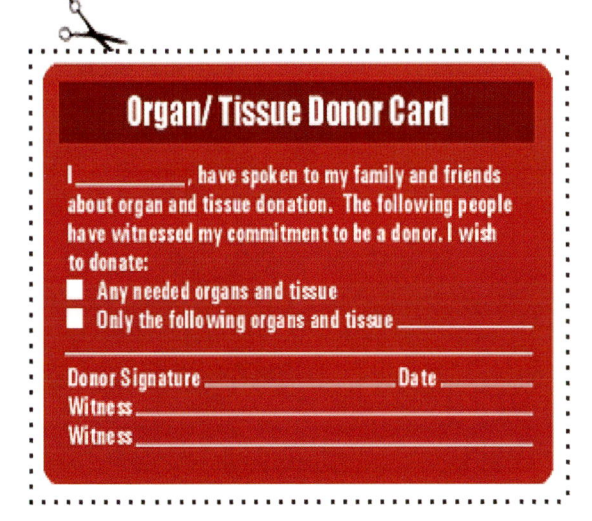

Organ/ Tissue Donor Card

I_____, have spoken to my family and friends about organ and tissue donation. The following people have witnessed my commitment to be a donor. I wish to donate:
- ■ Any needed organs and tissue
- ■ Only the following organs and tissue _____

Donor Signature _____ Date _____
Witness _____
Witness _____

I am   /
-
I am not

in Possession of a Donor Card

In case of an Emergency, please contact:

_____

_____

Doctors Number: ....
Doctors Name: ....
Address: ....
....
....
Blood Group: ....
Specific Medications: ....
....
Allergies:
....
....

Dentists Number: ....
Dentists Name: ....
Address:
....
....
....
....

Glasses prescription:
Left..
Right: ....

Annual Dates to Remember...

January
1st New Years Day

February
14th St. Valentine's Day

March
1st St. David's Day
17th St. Patrick's Day

April
1st April Fool's Day
23rd St. George's Day

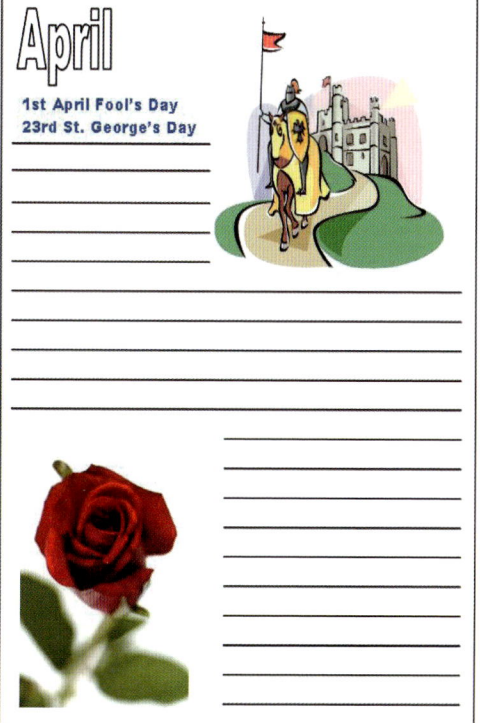

Annual Dates to Remember...

May
1st May Day

June
21st Summer Solstice

July
4th American Independence

August

Annual Dates to Remember...

September
Back to school / university

October
31st Halloween

Clocks go BACKWARD 1 Hour

November
5th Bonfire Night

December
22nd Winter Solstice
24th Christmas Eve
25th Christmas Day
26th Boxing Day
31st New Year's Eve

Firsts

My first car

Model: _____
Registration number: _____
Date bought/received: _____
Price: _____

My first day of independence

Date: _____
What I did: _____
_____
_____

My first home

Date: _____
Address: _____
_____

My first major purchase

I bought: _____
Price: _____
Store: _____
Date _____

My first independent holiday

Where: _____
When: _____
With: _____

Surveying A Property

Before you start looking for a house it is wise to put a **ceiling** on your price (a maximum amount you are going to spend). Always buy with your head and not your heart. This is the biggest financial decision you will make in your life, your first property purchase. You could make a mistake that you would find hard to recover from.

Be a nuisance, inspect everything, it is too late when you have moved in and find you have all the time in the world to discover faults. If you do find faults inform your solicitors, this is your guarantee of making sure things are right. Point out to the seller your observations, they possibly may not know but worst of all they may be trying to hide things. It is better to find out these things now when mistakes can be rectified or a price adjustment made. Believe me you have no chance when money has changed hands and you have moved in.

Choosing where you want to live is very important.
- With children in mind, is it near good schools?
- How will you get to work?
- Public transport or do you need close parking?

Finding a property is comparatively easy. Local newspapers carry extensive advertisements for housing. Contact as many estate agents as possible and ask to be put on their mailing list. Always be aware that the estate agent is employed to sell the property to you. The only money they make is by charging commissions on sales, without sales they cannot exist, so you know where their priorities lie!

Check weekly with the agents, the property you have been looking for could have just come on the market that week. Fate seems to sometimes play a big part in house purchase. Also when you have made an appointment to view a property keep the appointment and if possible, try to get there earlier before the agent, especially if the property is empty.

At this point it is worth considering the differences between ==freehold== and ==leasehold.==
With freehold you own any buildings and land up to the borders of the adjoining properties. Don't worry too much about this, as your solicitor will look after your interest into where the lines begin and end. These will be shown to you at your meeting with your solicitor.

Leasehold is where someone else owns the land, which your building is on. Most leases last between 99 and 999 years, your solicitor will inform you of how long the lease has yet to run, on a lease say of 99 years with 50 years since the original lease was signed leaving 49 years, you may find it more difficult to get a mortgage as the whole of the site reverts to the lease holder after the 49 years is up. The lease does not revert to 99 years every time there is a change in ownership of this property. Most houses are freehold but quite a lot of flats are leasehold so extra care should be taken. Keep in mind it could be much harder to get a mortgage on leasehold property.

On your first visit to view the property you should take into account the surrounding area. Your neighbours, bus stops, works or business premises, this could all affect the price.

You should then spend a lot of time inspecting the outside of the property, obviously your surveyor will point out major problems but take notes of all other problems you may see and pass on to your solicitor who can then get written guarantees to rectify any disagreements.

Main causes for concern can be:
- *Check for roof slates or tiles missing*
- *Is the chimney in good repair?*
- *Is the guttering old or in need of repair?*
- *Look for stains down the walls and cracks and bulges*
- *Is the mortar dry and in need of re-pointing? (This can be very expensive.)*
- *Look at window frames for signs of rot*
- *Evidence of recent painting to cover up defects*

Even if evidence of any of the above is found don't be dismayed if these are pointed out to the seller, a price adjustment can be arranged but all documented through your solicitor. Verbal contracts are not good enough. Viewing the outside is just as important. Don't laugh but binoculars are a great way to spot faults. If there is a ladder available be brave enough to make use of it, check flue outlets for extensive wear and tear.

Inside the Property

- *Look at the décor, is it old or new? If new is something being covered? A coat of paint can cover a multitude of sins.*
- *Do the kitchen units need replacing?*
- *Is the bathroom suite modern?*
- *You must look at the electric fittings and wiring, if these need attention it is not just a simple case of rewiring.*
- *Plastering and decoration can be just as expensive*
- *If carpets are to be sold in the sale, lift and look at the state of the underlay.*
- *Coverings on wood floors should be lifted for evidence of rot*

This is where you can make or lose thousands. The more information you have the better your negotiating position. Some points to consider:

- *How long has the property been on the market?*
- *How desperate are they to sell?*
- *Is the property empty?*
- *Are the sellers in a 'chain'?*
- *Has anyone let them down?*
- *Why are they selling the property?*
- *Is the property 'in need of redecoration or modernisation'?*

BE PREPARED TO HAGGLE.

All the above points are reasons that could lower your offer. Don't be embarrassed about offering perhaps 10, 20 even 30 per cent below the price the sellers are asking for. Even if the seller refuses your offer you can bide your time and keep looking for other properties.

If you are buying a new property try asking for a discount, it is not like buying something from a shop even if new there is always room for haggling and developers can do deals with you that they can't with private companies. Developers these days are amazed when prospective buyers don't ask for substantial discounts or improvements in the fixtures and fittings. Don't be put of, always act with confidence. Tell them a competitor has offered various incentives.

See if you can get help with the deposit, solicitor's fees, stamp duty or extras like kitchen appliances and carpets.
Don't be too anxious, relax when you are face to face and always keep in mind, there are thousands of properties you can purchase.
The seller can only see 1 or 2 buyers unless it is an exceptional property in which case it will be reflected in the price.

Always leave a door open, never say that's my final offer and I will not negotiate any further unless you have been talking for months and have exhausted all compromises.

Sometimes little things like you will endeavour to

complete quicker, will just tip the balance. A sale is not a sale until contracts are signed and deposits paid.

When you make your offer it will be subject to a contract, a survey and that you agree to buy providing there are no hidden faults, that the surveyor confirms the price is near enough right and that your solicitor sees no legal problems.

TYPES OF HOUSING SOCIAL LANDORDS

To rent accommodation from a council or Housing Association you will need to fill in an application form. However, this type of accommodation is allocated in different ways and largely depends on your current accommodation.

PRIVATE RENTED

This accommodation can be more expensive than social housing. Deposits and rent can be required in advance and often your renting, or tenancy as it is called, may only be for a short period at a time, such a six months.

Also, if you were to claim housing benefit it could be restricted depending on your circumstances and size of property.
In some places this kind of housing is easy to find and quick to move in to. But remember to be careful before you sign any agreements.

SHARED HOUSING

This includes joint tenancy/separate tenancy/multiple occupation. Your rights will differ depending on which agreement you have and who you live with. As a joint tenant you each have the same rights but in some cases you may have to pay your housemate's rent if he fails to. Sharing may be a great way to afford rent but it important to make a firm agreement on how the bills will be paid before you move in.

WHERE TO FIND SOMEWHERE

Finding somewhere to live that suits your needs is never easy. There is no magic formula to finding the right place. Sometimes it can take a lot of time, money and effort, while at other times you could simply be lucky and be in the right place at the right time.

If you want to Move…

If you are moving because you want to leave your current home, make sure you give yourself plenty of time to find somewhere else. Having plenty of time can increase the number of options you can choose from, and you won't feel pressurised into taking a place you are not really happy with.

Is your landlord putting you under pressure?
If you have to leave your home because the landlord says they want you out, make sure you know your rights.

The landlord will have to go through a certain procedure if they want you to leave. If they just throw you out, harass you, or put you under pressure to make you leave, they could be committing a criminal offence. You will probably have the right to stay for long enough for you to find another place. If you want to know what your rights are, get advice. If your landlord is putting you under pressure, you can get advice.

What Sorts of Housing Are Available?

There are many organisations involved in providing housing for people. You will improve your chances of finding the place that best suits you if you are aware of all the different options available. Some may not fit your needs, or be beyond your budget – but it's worth considering all the different alternatives.

Local Authority/Social Landlords

Advantages
- You will not have to pay a deposit
- Low cost contents insurance is available

- In some areas you will be able to move in straight away
- You will be given an, 'introductory tenancy' when you first move in. As long as you stick to the terms of this tenancy, after a year you will be given a 'secure tenancy'. This entitles you to stay in the property for as long as you wish, as long as you stick to the tenancy agreement
- You will have a publicly accountable landlord, with performance standards on such matters as carrying out repairs

Disadvantages

- You may not be able to live where you would like to – Local Authority may have nothing appropriate in the area you want
- There can be long waiting times for some areas
- Most Council houses and flats are unfurnished

Housing Associations

These provide homes for a wide range of people. They don't have many properties and this can mean long waiting lists in most areas

MORTGAGES

A mortgage is just another name for a loan and the lender takes what is known as a charge on the property through the deeds, which are held by the lender until the loan is paid. Re-payment is usually by 1 or 2 methods:

Endowment mortgage is where you agree to repay the loan at the end of a fixed period. Throughout the mortgage your monthly payments pay the interest on the original loan.

The capital is re-paid by means of an assurance policy which when it matures repays the loan. Any profit made by the policy then goes to you, but unfortunately over recent years have received a bad press due to policy maturing and not having earned enough to repay the loan.
This type of mortgage is not for the fainthearted but more for the speculator, you're probably best giving this one a miss.

The most popular mortgage is a **Repayment mortgage**, which is the simplest. You borrow a fixed amount for a set period. The loan is reduced monthly by your payments. At the beginning of the mortgage most of your repayments are paying off interest but as the years go on you will see the outstanding loan come down dramatically.

You must take into account that the mortgage repayments will start one month after completion whether you have taken up residence or not.

What to take with you

When you first talk about a mortgage with an adviser, he or she will help you work out a practical personal budget – so it's a good idea to take a few details of your finances.

- Details of your current income (take two recent salary slips if possible)
- Your last P60 form (certificate of pay and tax deducted)
- Information on any savings you have (take your savings book for example)
- An indication of the value of your current home, if you will be selling it before buying another
- List of any other regular outgoing payments, including household bills
- Details of your current mortgage, if you have one, (a recent mortgage statement is ideal) and any endowment policies you may have
- If you're self-employed, we'll need to see copies of your last three years' business accounts (accountant's certificate, profit and loss account, and balance sheet)
- If you are a director and major shareholder in a limited company, we will need copies of the last three years' full audited accounts (not modified accounts) of the company

Some of the best home bargains are found at auction. This is an organised event where people will meet to 'bid' for a house – in other words offer a certain amount for a house and if no one is prepared to offer more money they 'win' the house and it is sold to them.

If someone offers a larger amount than them they have been 'outbid' and will not be able to buy the house unless they put in a better offer.

To 'outbid' a person's offer you need to offer more money than they are willing to pay for the house.

Houses that are available for auction are not advertised in the usual way though sometimes they may be advertised in the paper.

To view the properties available for auction in the area you wish to buy (extremely important) you will need to contact the relevant organisations that hold the events some of which are listed on the next page.

You can get into big trouble if you buy a house at auction before viewing it to see if there are any problems with it!

Buying at auction is a risky business so I would recommend that you attend a few practice auctions before putting in a serious bid.

TIP: Some sellers will take offers before the auction even begins!

If you wish to get more details of upcoming house auctions in the area you wish to buy in you might want to look at:

- www.auctionpropertyforsale.co.uk
- www.ukpad.com
- www.propertyauctions.com

TENANCY AGREEMENT

There are various different kind of tenancy. Your rights depend on what kind you have. The law in this area is complicated-you may need to get advice. What follows is only a basic guide.

What rights you have depend on three factors:
Whether or not you pay rent and have the right to occupy the accommodation as your own.
- Whether or not you share where you live with your landlord.
- The date you moved in.

DO YOU PAY RENT? CAN YOU CALL THE PLACE YOUR OWN?

Some people don't have a tenancy at all: - They have what is called a 'license'.
For example, if you go to stay with friends over the weekend, you have a license to be there. If you are sleeping on your friend's sofa, you have a license to be there: - You rent a room in a bed and breakfast establishment and someone comes in to clean the room and change the sheets.

If you have a license, you have fewer rights than someone with a tenancy. Because of this some landlords will tell you that you have a license, when you really have a tenancy. If you have any doubts where you stand, contact your local Citizen Advice Centre.

DO YOU SHARE WHERE YOU LIVE WITH YOUR LANDLORD?

If you live with your landlord you have fewer rights than you would otherwise.

WHEN DID YOU MOVE IN?

If you pay rent, call the place your own, and the landlord doesn't live with you, you will have a tenancy. What sort you have depends on when you moved in. If you moved in after 15th January 1997, you are likely to have an a*ssured* tenancy.

If you have moved in before 28th February 1997, you are likely to have an *assured* tenancy or an *assured short* hold tenancy.

- If the landlord gave you a section 20 notice before you moved in and you tenancy is for a fixed period of at least 6 months, you have an assured tenancy.
- If your landlord did not give you a document, or your tenancy is not for a fixed period, you have an assured tenancy.
- If you have been with your present landlord since before 15 January 1989, then you may have a *protected* tenancy. If you think this might apply to you, get advice.

WHAT IF YOU HAVE NOTHING IN WRITING

Assured tenancies do not last for a set period of time. The tenancy carries on until the landlord goes through the legal procedure to get you to leave.

IF THE LANDLORD WANTS YOU TO GO...

The landlord will have to follow a set legal procedure if they want you to leave the property-they can't just throw you out.

When you pay your rent get something in writing. If you pay your rent weekly, you are entitles to a rent book-the landlord writes in this whenever you pay your rent.

If you don't pay weekly, request a rent book-or buy one yourself, and ask the landlord to sign it when they collect the rent. If you don't have a rent book, ask for a receipt whenever you pay your rent. Keep any records you can that you have paid, such as cheque or postal order stubs. If Housing Benefit pays your rent, you could ask them to confirm what they have paid.

IF YOU FALL BEHIND WITH THE RENT...

Talk to the landlord as soon as you can. If you cannot pay off all that you owe, offer to pay a little extra each week or month towards the missing payments, if you can manage to. Don't leave it too long before you talk to the landlord, or they go to court and you could lose your home. If they do go to court, they might also get an order against you, which means you could have trouble getting credit in the future.

CAN THE LANDLORD INCREASE YOUR RENT?

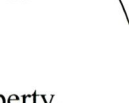

The landlord must follow a set procedure if they want to increase the rent. In general they should let you know in writing that they want to do this 4 weeks in advance.

Your rights depend on when you moved in to the property.

If you moved in to the property after 15th January 1989:

If you disagree with the rent increase, it may be possible to appeal to an independent body called the Rent Assessment Committee. This will depend on the sort of tenancy agreement you have. There are various rules the landlord has to follow if they want to increase the rent. Get the advice before you sign a new agreement or pay a rent increase-once you have signed, or paid the higher rent, you cannot object to the increase.

If you have moved in to the property before 15th January 1989:

You might have an informal agreement, without anything on paper. If this is the case, and you moved in after 28th February 1997, you will probably have an *assured tenancy*.

TENANCY AGREEMENTS

Tenancy agreements are often wordy and are divided up into many separate parts called 'clauses' Do not sign the agreement until you have read it and are sure that you understand all the parts.

Ask the landlord if you can have a copy to take away before you sign it. As soon as you do sign the agreement it becomes a contract.

This means it is a legally binding agreement between both you and the landlord and that both parties will stick to what is written in the agreement.

The landlord adds their details to a pre-printed form. Make sure that the details that the landlord has written are correct - such as your name, the address, the date of tenancy starts, how long it lasts, the landlord's phone number, and so on.

The law says that the landlord has certain responsibilities-for example, there are some repairs that a landlord must carry out. This is still the case regardless of what is written on the tenancy agreement. A landlord cannot write in an agreement that a tenant has to do all the repairs - they would be trying to get out of their legal responsibilities if they did so! If you think a landlord has written something unreasonable in a tenancy agreement, consult a housing adviser for advice.

If there is anything in the agreement you are unhappy about, discuss it with the landlord. You can ask them to change the agreement before you sign.

HOW LONG DOES THE TENANCY AGREEMENT LAST?

An **Assured Shorthold** tenancy may run from week to week or month to month until further notice, or it may last for a specific period of time of not less than 6 months. Be careful if you agree to rent somewhere for a particular period like 6 or 12 months, or even 5 years or ten years.
You are agreeing to pay the rent until the end of this period…even if you move out. Make sure there is an option written into the agreement to say that you can leave before this time if you give notice.

If you rent somewhere for a specific period of time, you do not necessarily have to go when that time has expired. You can stay in the property until the landlord goes through the legal procedure to get you to leave. Or the landlord may ask you to sign a new agreement to stay for a further set period of time.

You may have the right to a Fair Rent. A Fair Rent is set by an independent official called a Rent Officer. It is the most a landlord is allowed to charge. If a landlord wants to increase a Fair Rent, there is a set procedure which they have to follow.

VISITS FROM THE LANDLORD

In general the landlord does not have the right to come in to the property whenever they like - they should let you know in advance when they are going to call, preferably 24 hours in advance and in writing. The landlord does not have the right to use keys to enter the property whenever they want.

Obviously, the landlord may have perfectly valid reasons for entering the property.

They may be entitled to a set of keys so they can get in to the property in case of an emergency- though you should be aware that they have the keys and in agreement to the landlord using them in an emergency. They may also need to get in to the property to see if repair work needs to be carried out.

On the other hand, if the landlord behaves in such a way that you cannot live in peace in your own home, they may be breaking the law.

In Relations an emergency, you can get advice and help from the Tenancy Officer Service. You will need to have your landlord's address and phone numbers so that you can get in touch with them easily- for example, if there are any problems where you live, or let them know if you want to leave.

You have a legal right to know your landlord's name and address-if you don't, ask the person who collects the rent. They must give you a contact name and address in England and Wales.

The only safe way to double your money is to fold it in half.

REPAIRS

Sorting out repairs to a property is one of the most common sources of problems between landlords and tenants. It is important that you know, right from the start of your tenancy which repairs your landlord is responsible for and how you should properly report them. It is the landlord's responsibility to do basic repairs to the building. This includes repairs to the structure and the exterior of the building.

For example, a leaky roof, badly fitted or rotting windows and doors, rising damp etc.

This also includes:
Repairs to drains, gutters and external pipes
Repairs to baths, sinks and toilets
Repairs to the heating and to the water heating
General building repairs

Repairs that need doing due to damage caused by someone with no connection to you - for example if damage occurs during a break in or damage caused by another family's children playing in the street.

If a repair needs doing, tell the landlord as soon as possible. Do this in writing, and keep a copy as proof that the landlord is aware of the repair work required, they usually have no responsibility to do anything about it. Make sure you have a number to contact your landlord in case of an emergency- for example if you have a burst pipe.

If the landlord does not do the repairs, there are various things you can do to sort the situation out.

You should get advice about which is best in your situation.
Do not stop paying the rent in order to force the landlord to do the repairs.
This could put you in a situation where you lose your home.

Your responsibilities:

As a tenant you have to look after the property in a reasonable and responsible way. You are responsible for minor, day-to-day repairs such as cleaning windows, replacing fuses or unblocking waste pipes.
If you or your visitors cause any damage it is up to you to put it right.
Your landlord has the right to check for disrepair:

Your landlord has the right to check your home for disrepair. They must give you at least 24 hours notice, in writing that they are coming to carry out an inspection and they must come at a reasonable time of the day. Obviously, if a repair needs doing urgently, it will probably not be in your interest to insist on your rights regarding notice of visit and you would be best off allowing the landlord to visit immediately.

If the landlord doesn't do the repairs

Once you have let the landlord know about the repair, you have to give them a reasonable chance to do the work before you take the matter further. There are a few hard and fast rules about how long a landlord can take to do repairs-but they have to take into account the sort of repair it is. For example unblocking a toilet is more urgent than say a damp proof course.
Often tenants stop paying their rent when their landlords fail to carry out repairs.
This can lead to more problems than it solves, as stated previously, could even result in you losing your home. **GET ADVICE!**

IF YOUR LANDLORD WANTS YOU TO LEAVE

IS THE LANDLORD HARASSING YOU?

Your landlord must follow procedures if they want you to leave. If they harass you in an attempt to make you leave, they may be committing a criminal offence.

Harassment may include:
- Violence or threats of violence
- Calling round late at night
- Coming into where you live without
- Having arranged to call round
- Cutting off the water, gas or electricity

Report any harassment to your local housing authority, they will be only too pleased to help and advise you. If the harassment gets too severe or even life threatening, ring your local police.

INVENTORY

Get your landlord to make a list of the contents in your property. The list should include information of the property and of its contents-for example, it should state if anything is faulty. Ask your landlord to sign the list, make one yourself. Get a friend or relative to sign as a witness to say the list is accurate!

ADDRESS:

I confirm that the list attached is an accurate record of items included in the tenancy offered at the above address.

DATED:

Inventory

Ask your landlord to sign the list, sign it yourself and keep a copy. If your landlord won't make a list, make one yourself. Get a friend or relative to sign as a witness to say that it is accurate.

INVENTORY

Address: _____
_____
_____

I confirm that the list below is an accurate record of items included in the tenancy offered at the above address.
The tenancy is dated: _____

Condition

KITCHEN

	Good	Fair	Poor
_____	☐	☐	☐
_____	☐	☐	☐
_____	☐	☐	☐

LIVING ROOM

	Good	Fair	Poor
_____	☐	☐	☐
_____	☐	☐	☐
_____	☐	☐	☐

BEDROOM

	Good	Fair	Poor
_____	☐	☐	☐
_____	☐	☐	☐
_____	☐	☐	☐

OTHER

	Good	Fair	Poor
_____	☐	☐	☐
_____	☐	☐	☐
_____	☐	☐	☐

Signed: _____   _____   _____
          Landlord/Agent   Tenant/Licensee   Witness

SECURITY

Some of us are absolutely fine with living alone, as long as we always know where the baseball bat is located, we can relax. But for those who maybe haven't lived completely alone before it can be a hard adjustment.

Hearing all those new creaks and strange sounds can take some getting used to, for complete peace of mind taking care of your security will most definitely help you to settle.

The biggest crime is your own memory. How often do you forget to lock doors and windows? A lot of thieves rely on chance, seeing an open window or open door. I know accidents will happen, but check and double check!

-**Never** leave a hidden key anywhere outside property. This is a silly idea and your best choice if your notorious for leaving keys is a trustworthy neighbor or a key safe.

-**Mark valuables**. Marking your valuables increases the chance of stolen goods being returned.

-**Always be aware** of your fire exits and keep them clear. Think about trees etc hanging near to second level windows? Could this assist a burglar?

-One little handy tip is to put plant pots on the window edges. The last thing a burglar wants is to create noise and attract attention to themselves!

The risk of someone breaking into a house in your area is higher than it used to be but this doesn't mean that a break-in has to happen to you. It does mean that you need to have certain types of locks and security devices fitted to your home such as those below. You can improve your security in general by fitting deadlocks and/or bolts on external doors. A porch light and spy hole/door viewer will also give you that extra piece of mind.

Locks

-Main Entrance Door
This should have a lock which can be locked from both the inside and outside

-Double Doors/French Doors or Windows
These must have two security bolts that are locked with a key that are fitted at both the top and bottom of the doors.

-Other Doors
Must have either a lock which can be locked from both the inside and outside like a main entrance door or have the same two security bolts that are locked with a key fitted at both the top and bottom of the doors like all double doors should have.

-Sliding Doors
These must have either the lock that can be locked from both the inside and outside, or the two security bolts that are locked with a key and fitted at both the top and bottom of the doors, or have what is known as an anti-lift device and a patio key lock.

-Windows
Any window that could potentially be reached by a burglar without a ladder must be locked by window key lock devices.

-Louvre Windows
All glass in a window must be secured with the right type of glue in their frames.

It is necessary to use all these devices:
- Whenever there is no person in charge of your home within the land belonging to the home
- When you go to bed at night

IF YOU LIVE WITH OTHER PEOPLE, DON'T LEAVE IT TO THEM TO CHECK, FAR BETTER THAT ALL OF YOU GET INTO A RITUAL EVERY NIGHT TO MAKE SURE THAT EVERYTHING IS SECURE AND SAFE.

This is a guide to the 'stop and search' procedures. It does not cover all the law.

WHAT IS A STOP AND SEARCH?

Police officers can stop and talk to you at any time. But they should only search you if they suspect you are carrying:

Drugs
Weapons

Stolen property

Or tools that could be used to commit a crime

WHY ME?

If we are stopped and\or searched it doesn't mean you have done something wrong. But a Police officer must have a good reason for stopping you and should tell you what this is.
You should not be stopped and\or searched just because of your age, race, colour or the way you dress.

WHERE CAN I BE STOPPED AND\OR SEARCHED?

In a public place, or anywhere if the police believe you have committed a serious crime.
If the police think there may be serious violence then they can search everyone in an area for weapons – for example near a football ground – without needing a good reason to search each person.

A police officer can stop a vehicle at any time and ask to see the driver's license and other documents.

If they have good reason to think your car contains stolen goods, drugs or weapons, they could search it – even if you are not there. But the police must leave a notice saying that they have.

If the search causes damage, you can ask for compensation but only if they didn't find anything to connect you to a crime.

HOW WILL THEY SEARCH ME?

Before searching you the police officer must normally tell you:

- *Their name,*
- *The station they work at,*
- *Why they chose you and*
- *What they are looking for.*

If the police officer is not in uniform they must show you their identity card.

If you are in a public place, you only have to take off:

Your coat or jacket and your gloves.

(NOTE: If a more thorough search is required it could mean a trip to the station however if you can find a suitable private place the search could be carried out here, saving you time.)

The police can only ask you to take off more than this including anything you wear for religious reasons, such as a face scarf, if they take you somewhere private, for example a police station.

This does not mean you are being arrested; in this case the officer who searches you must be of the same sex as you.

WHAT HAPPENS NEXT?

If you are stopped and\or searched, the police officer should write it down unless there are exceptional circumstances which prevent a record being given. The copy will contain the following:

- *Your name or a description of you;*
- *Why they searched you;*
- *Where and when they searched you;*
- *What they were looking for and anything they found;*
- *The name and number of the officer who searched you;*
- *The police station the officer is based at and*
- *Your ethnic background as defined by you.*

Like or loathe the police, there is no alternative. They reflect the society we live in and so therefore have the same feelings and foibles as the general public. Your best advice is to be as cooperative as possible. Attitude will only bring out the worst in them just as it would with you.

Bailiffs

What is a bailiff?

If you are honest with your creditors and attempt to pay your debts, you shouldn't have much trouble. If you try to avoid paying your debts and don't communicate with your creditors, this is where the problems can start.

Some collection agencies will threaten to send someone to your door if you won't pay up, however generally this will NOT be a bailiff, but a representative of a Debt Collection Agency. This is very different, as a representative has no powers at all.

A bailiff, on the other hand, is someone authorised by the courts to collect a debt on behalf of a creditor (someone you owe money to).

How can I tell if it is a bailiff?

Bailiffs should provide identification or authorisation if you ask them to. Bailiffs collecting for rent must show their certificate from the county court, and those collecting unpaid council tax must show written authorisation from the local authority if you ask them too.

What can a bailiff do?

Different bailiffs have different powers when it comes to debt collection and each collects various types of debt. There are county courts, private and certificated bailiffs to name a few, and whilst each is different there are certain rules they must all adhere to.

THE RULES

When can bailiffs come around?

Whilst bailiffs collecting rent are only allowed to call between sunset and sunrise all other bailiffs can call AT ANY TIME, although it should be at a time considered 'reasonable', usually between 8am and 8pm.

Can bailiffs force their way into my house, or do I have to let them in?

Although in rare cases bailiffs from the Collector of Taxes (Inland Revenue) can get a warrant to force entry in to your home, as a general rule bailiffs are not allowed to force entry into your home and have a right to peaceful entry only, which means whilst they can't break down the door, they can let themselves in through an open door or window. Therefore, if all of your doors and windows are locked, a bailiff cannot enter peaceably. It's also worth remembering that you can't be arrested for not letting a bailiff in.

Initial Entry

Once bailiffs have entered your home the first time, they are able to return without your permission, and can break in to enter your home again. Their initial entry, therefore, is very important to them.

Once inside you property a bailiff is allowed to go into any room and even break open any cupboard that is locked inside. They will then attempt to seize goods to the value of your debt, and will indicate this verbally or by marking or touching the item(s). These goods will be sold at public auction, but if they make more money than you owe (including any additional fees incurred by the bailiffs etc) you are entitled to the difference.

Ways a bailiff may try to gain peaceful entry
- Through an open door or window
- Asking to use the telephone
- Asking to discuss matters inside
- Attempting to walk in the door as soon as it is opened (although they are NOT allowed to force their way past someone at the door).

Goods that cannot be seized by bailiffs

Bailiffs acting on behalf of the magistrates' court cannot seize:

- clothing, beds and bedding tools of the trade
- any provisions necessary to satisfy the basic domestic needs of the family (clothing, bedding etc). This would also normally include fridge, cookers, freezers, but may not include video recorders, second TV's, jewelry, washing machines, stereos or microwave cookers.

All other bailiffs cannot seize:

- tools, goods, vehicles and other items of equipment necessary for use by you in your employment, business or vocation;
- clothing, bedding, furniture, household equipment and provisions as are necessary for satisfying the basic domestic needs of you and your family

What if they try and take something that isn't mine?

Bailiffs are not allowed to take goods that do not belong to the debtor or are subject to hire purchase or conditional sale agreements. However, they can take goods that are jointly owned by the debtor and another person, but if they are eventually sold they must pay the other person their share of the money.

Complaints against bailiffs

Occasionally, the bailiff may do something wrong or act beyond their powers. For example, if they;
- harass you or other people in the property
- threaten arrest or imprisonment
- use offensive language
- cause damage to your belongings

When this happens and the bailiffs do something wrong, there are various ways of making a complaint;

1. First, you should try complaining to the bailiff's firm.
2. If this is unsuccessful you can take the complaint to the creditor for whom the bailiff is acting. It may be necessary for you to follow through with your creditor's formal complaints procedure and any codes of practice, should they have them.
3. If you are still not happy, you can pursue the matter by contacting the bailiffs' professional or trade organisation. All have the power to discipline the bailiff and they can award compensation.
4. Finally, you could choose to take legal action against a bailiff in the county court, and in this case it is possible that the issue of a Claim will prompt the bailiff into settling without the need and expense of actually having to attend court.

To make enquiries about your legal position regarding a complaint about a bailiff it may be helpful to contact your local free advice centre.

Once a Bailiff has called to your home the debt escalates and shoots upwards and upwards. Try to avoid this at all costs. But the same rules apply.

COUNTY COURT JUDGEMENTS

Financial worries such as APR and student loans are sometimes inevitable when leaving home. It is how you cope with this debt that will determine possible C.C.J's arising. County Court Judgements or C.C.J's as they are commonly known, are not only very disturbing but highly expensive. You not only have to pay the debt but also the Court's officers. Plus Bailiffs can swell the debt until it becomes unrecognisable from the original sum.

The obvious thing is not to get into debt in the first place. But once you are, you have to deal with it. I can promise you that the problem will not go away! The first rule is to attend the Court hearing, or the very least reply to the Court papers that are served on you.

!!!! Don't be frightened of the Court Officers…they are there to help you!!!!

In Court you will be asked about your financial circumstances and to provide as much evidence regarding your outgoings as you possibly can. If judgement is found against you it is most important that you comply with the decision. The consequences, if you don't, can be dire.

A further side to this is that all banks, Building Societies and hire purchase companies have immediate access to the Registry of County Court Judgements. If your name is listed, the consequences are most unwelcome

In many cases, the Courts can order an employer to deduct money from your wages. (Subject to Protected Earnings Orders). Other methods of enforcements are also available including charges on properties.

WHAT EMPLOYERS CAN DO!

It is increasingly common practice for employers to have an applicant's credit status checked. If you decide to change jobs, a Judgement in your name will not help. Having a judgement made against you and finding you cannot keep up the payments, (that's if you asked for the time to pay) need not be the end of the world. Do not be deceived into thinking that the problems of this nature go away. If you find that you cannot settle in full immediately-make an offer.

Sensible offers will be considered sympathetically-provided they are backed up with a bankers order or post-dated cheques.

Solicitors

It is best to go to a Solicitor that has been recommended to you but they can be found in most town centres. Yellow Pages and Thompson's have full lists of Solicitors in your area.

Preparing to Contact a Solicitor

The more preparation you do before the interview, the more you'll get out of it:

1) Write down all the questions that you want to ask, and take the list along to the interview

2) Get together all the relevant paperwork you'll need in your meeting. Try to get any letters or documents organised by date before you attend the interview as this will help your solicitor to understand your situation and advise you more quickly

3) If you are planning to take someone with you, mention this when you are making the appointment

Meeting Your Solicitor

- At the beginning of the meeting, ask how long the meeting will last so you can plan how to fit in all your points in this time
- Use the list of questions you made in advance. Make sure you ask all your questions and understand all the answers you are given. If there is anything you don't understand ask the Solicitor to explain
- Try to answer your Solicitor's questions as clearly and accurately as you can but be prepared the Solicitor will probably ask you many questions
- Show your Solicitor any relevant documents you have brought with you
- Ask you Solicitor to send you a letter summarising the advice you've been given

Solicitors Charges

Your Solicitor must make it clear to you as soon as possible the way in which she or he will work on your case. It may be that you will be eligible for *publicly funded assistance.*

Paying for legal services

It is a solicitor's responsibility to keep you informed of costs and to give you a clear bill showing what has been done and the amount charged.

Advice on Legal Aid

The Legal Services Commission is responsible for The Community Legal Service and the Criminal Defence Service that funds advice and representation for criminal charges. These funded services are only available from solicitors or advice agencies that are controlled by the Legal Services Commission. This means they have been checked to make sure they meet certain criteria and provide good service.

How do I qualify for Legal Aid?

For civil matters, you may qualify for free legal advice and assistance. If you meet certain financial criteria, and your case is of a type covered by the legal aid scheme. If you do not meet them you may be asked to pay a contribution towards your legal advice.

In criminal matters, legal advice and representation at the police station is free to everyone and court advice and representation is free if the case is judged to be serious; other assistance may be asked to pay a contribution to your legal advice cost if your case progresses.

No Win, No Fee Arrangements

Apart from Family or Criminal matters, many types of claim are suitable for what is commonly known as 'no win, no fee'.

If your claim is successful

In a 'no win, no fee' agreement your solicitor will only be paid if the claim is successful. He or she may be entitled to an extra fee (known as a success fee). The losing party pays both the basic fee and this extra fee in full or part.

If there are other incurred costs such as court fees or the fee for a medical report the losing party should pay for these.

You are liable to pay your solicitor for any costs that the losing party is not ordered to pay.

If your claim fails

You will not have to pay your own solicitor, but you will still probably have to pay the costs for the other side. Also, you will have to pay any other incurred costs (such as court fees or reports). These are normally known as disbursements. However, your Solicitor will normally have arranged for you to have insurance to cover this risk. This is known as 'after the event' insurance. You may have to pay a premium.

For a 'no win, no fee' arrangement to be valid, the solicitor has to complete a number of forms at various stages.

Complaints about Solicitors

Consumer Complaints Service

The Consumer Complaints Service is the part of the Law Society which helps you of you have a problem with your solicitor.
They deal with:
- Complaints from clients about poor service
- Applications for remuneration certificates (where we check your Solicitor's bill is fair)

We also receive reports about professional misconduct by Solicitors.
The Consumer Complaints Service Helpline number is **0845 608 6565**
Lines are open from 9 to 5, Monday to Friday.

This service is monitored by an Independent Commisioner, Sir Stephen Lander.

BANKING

BEING BROKE IS NO JOKE!

Having no money and struggling to get by is not a great way to live, as I'm sure plenty of you know. Alright, so you can call your parents for one of those loans, but exactly how many times can you do this? It has probably been your decision to leave and now you're out to prove something.

Firstly, you will need your own bank account, if you don't have one already. You can do this at any local building society or bank; opening a 'current account' is your best option for a first account. This kind of account does not charge you for using services apart from when you commit the biggest sin of all which is when you go into the red i.e. 'overdrawn' without your bank's consent. Charges for this can be extreme.

Budgeting takes a lot of practice, making your money last and paying bills on time.

The best way is to plan carefully and a budgeting chart may be helpful. Bills can sometimes be spread out so you don't have to pay all at once while others need to be paid as soon as you get them. You can pay bills by bank, internet, direct debit, telephone, cheques or postal orders. There is usually a list of ways to pay on the back of your bill.

IF YOU DO GET INTO DIFFICULTY PLEASE DO NOT JUST IGNORE LETTERS SENT TO YOU FROM YOUR BANK, THE WORSE WILL BE FEARED IF YOU DO.

Simply- make an appointment as soon as possible and explain to them your circumstances and the problems you are having. They may be able to help you out.

A bank as well as being a profit-making organisation, is there to help you as their customer. They can only say no, or at least advise you on how best to resolve the matter. Never go to a 'loan shark'. These people are sometimes just short of being gangsters and at the risk of being sued…the television advert solving your money worries will only ever add to your difficulties. The interest rates are so sky high, you really will be giving them four or five times the amount they originally gave you. If unfortunately you do get into the clutches of these people you need to seek advice straight away.

Someone at the Citizens Advice Bureau will certainly try to help you.

So the basics you will need are: A bank account, a chequebook and a debit card. Choose carefully who to bank with.

See what sort of accounts there are and try not to be tempted by the free gifts that many banks offer today. Do some research and find the best deal for you!

DEBIT AND CREDIT:

Debit is money taken out of your account. Credit is money you borrow from the bank in order to pay back later.

DEBIT\SWITCH CARD:

A card for buying\paying for things and is used for taking cash from

your account.

CHEQUE BOOK

This is a written instruction by you, which instructs the bank to pay money on your behalf.

OVERDRAFT:

A facility agreed by you and the bank, which gives you access to more money than you have, you borrow a certain amount.

INTEREST:

Money added to your account by your bank.

BANK CHARGES:

These will apply, for example, if you go over your overdraft limit or send a cheque and there is no money in the account to pay for it.

Debit and Credit cards can be your best friend and sometimes may help you out of a tight fix. However, try to use them sensibly; again debt is always lurking round that corner waiting for you.

Remember- whether you buy a holiday or a can of beans, at the end of the month it all has to be paid for. To make them really work for you paying each month and on time is a must. Even one day late and you will not believe the interest you will pay back.

If you take advantage of cards that give you % or low interest you must be meticulous and completely certain of all your dealings.

Make sure you have paid off your loan before the agreed date of beneficial rates or have another credit company in place to take on the loan. The least you should try for is to pay back twice the minimum required or you will be in debt for years.

Always write in your cheque stubs the amount of the cheque and who it is paid to. Check these with your monthly statement for charges and always keep a tab on these payments. After all, it's your money and nobody else will check these details.

Build a relationship with your bank. They like a lot of organisations rely on track records, Don't try to con them. After all when in business for hundreds of years, every excuse in the book has been heard… hundreds of times…honesty is always the best policy and will get you much further!

Everyone looks for advice from the person they know, whom is going to tell them what they want to hear.

Bank Accounts

There are different types of bank accounts:

- <u>Cash Account</u>
- <u>Basic Bank Account</u>

- <u>Current Account</u>- you need to pay money into this type of account when opening it (how much will depend on the bank you choose so shop around). The back will give you a small amount of money called *Interest* each month as long as there is money in the account. How much *interest* you get in a Current Account depends on:
1. How much money you pay into the account in a year - even if it is taken out again
2. The *interest rate* of the account…the more money and the higher the interest rate, the more *interest* you will get.

- <u>Savings Account</u>- same as a Current Account but this is for when you want to store money for a long amount of time to save up for something big. The money you put into this type of account will gain you far more *interest* than a savings account. How much *interest* depends on:
1. How much money you put into the account
2. The Bank's *interest rate*
3. How long the money is left in the account…the more money and the higher the interest rate and the longer the money is left in the account, the more interest you will get.

- <u>High Interest Savings Account</u>-Same as a Savings Account but there is an even higher rate of interest. However there is often a limit to when you are allowed to withdraw money and how many times a year you are allowed to do it. Also you may need to pay in a larger amount to open the account than with other bank accounts. So only for serious savers!
- <u>High Interest Bonds</u>-same as a High Interest Savings Account but there is a very large amount required (usually in the £1000's) and the money cannot be removed for a very long period of time (usually at least 3 years). On the plus side the rate of these accounts is extremely high so there is a chance to make a lot of interest money.

Cheque Book

If your account includes a chequebook it will most likely be sent to your house a few days after you have opened your account. A cheque lets you give money without actually handing over cash (as long as you actually have that money in your account!). The cheque asks your bank to make the payment for you and take the money out of your account and give it to whoever you write immediately after the word 'Pay' on the cheque. This usually takes the bank 3-5 days.

sort code   account no.

You may be asked to show a cheque guarantee card when you give someone a cheque.

Once you've written and handed over a cheque the bank may still be able to 'stop' it though you will usually have to pay for them to do this. If you want a bank to stop a cheque you must either go into the branch itself tell them as soon as possible. You cannot stop a cheque if you have used a cheque guarantee card with it.

Budget

One of the best ways to budget is to plan carefully, listing all of your incoming money and your outgoings. Then, take the outgoings from the incoming money, see how much is left over and then decide whether to save it, or what to spend it on.

Income (monthly)

Wages	£_____
Benefits	£_____
Other	£_____
Total	£_____

Expenditure (monthly)

Rent	£_____
Council Tax	£_____
Water	£_____
Electricity	£_____
Telephone	£_____
TV License	£_____
Laundry	£_____
Food	£_____
Spending money	£_____
Clothes	£_____
Car/Transport	£_____
Insurance	£_____
Loans	£_____
Other debts	£_____
Total	£_____

Monthly Budget

£_____   **Total Monthly Income**

- £_____   **Total Monthly Expenditure**

=£_____   **Money Left Over (If you're lucky!)**

Cash or Credit?

DANGER!!! The true cost of APR.

Please, please seek advice, as different lenders calculate APR differently and you may end up repaying many times more than you borrowed. Below you will see how interest turns a small loan into a horrendous debt.

	January	February	March	April	May	June
Start Balance (without interest)	£1200	£1100	£1000	£900	£800	£700
Monthly Repayment	£100	£100	£100	£100	£100	£100
Monthly Interest (10%)	£120	£120	£120	£120	£120	£120
Total Monthly Repayment	£220	£220	£220	£220	£220	£220
End Balance	£1100	£1000	£900	£800	£700	£600

	July	Aug	Sept	October	Nov	Dec
Start Balance (without interest)	£600	£500	£400	£300	£200	£100
Monthly Repayment	£100	£100	£100	£100	£100	£100
Monthly Interest (10%)	£120	£120	£120	£120	£120	£120
Total Monthly Repayment	£220	£220	£220	£220	£220	£220
End Balance	£500	£400	£300	£200	£100	£0

Total borrowed: £1200

Initial loan repaid: £1200

Total interest paid: £1440

Total repaid: £2640

Dealing with Lost Credit Cards

What to Do if you lose your Credit Card

The following is a list of numbers to call if you lose your credit card, you must call as soon as possible.

Time is money!

It only takes seconds for a thief to draw money out of your account.

Your Credit Card company could dispute the amount that is withdrawn unless you use every endeavour to inform them of your loss. They will want you to provide evidence of where you were when the card was stolen and how easy or difficult for someone to gain access to it.

Never give anyone your card number…whether they are friends or not.

After stealing a credit card, thieves have even been known to pose as the police over the phone, to ask for someone's card number. If this happens ring the police as soon as possible.

Benefits of CardGuard

- They will cancel any lost or stolen cards and order replacements with just one free phone call.
- You'll be covered for up to £1,000 for your liabilities under the terms and conditions of your cards in case of fraudulent use, provided you notify us within 24 hours of discovering your cards are missing. After you've informed us, the cover is up to £50,000.
- Receive up to £1,500 per policyholder emergency cash advance if your cards are lost or stolen whilst away from home, and you simply repay it within 28 days.
- Once we've accepted your completed CardGuard application, the premium will be debited directly from the bank account you designate at the current rate until cancelled by you in writing.
- CardGuard is available with most Bank credit cards.

Another thing you can do to prevent loss if your card is stolen or lost is to register your card against online theft. There are quite a few banks that allow you to do this free of charge so that in the event of your card being lost/stolen any online transactions that you will not have to pay for any online transactions that are carried out without your consent. To register for these services you will usually have to have online banking which not all banks offer. However if they do if is a good idea to sign up not just for convenience but so that you can get your card protected.

Why not sign up for a service called 'Card guard'. Most banks offer a service of this type that you have to pay for each month but in the event of your card being stolen and money being taken it will cover you for a large amount usually around £50,000. It is basically extra insurance for your card should you lose it.

> **It's good to have money and the things that money can buy, but it's good to check once in a awhile and make sure that you haven't lost the things that money cannot buy.**

Emergency Credit Card Numbers

Abbey (and Cahoot)	UK 08459 724 724
Allied Irish Bank	Ireland 01668 5500
Alliance and Leicester	UK 0800 0688 638
American Express	UK 0800 521 313
Bank of Ireland	Ireland 1890 706 706
	Ireland 1890 251 251
Bank of Scotland:	UK 08457 20 30 99
Barclays Bank	UK 0808 100 6667
Barclaycard	UK 01604 230 230
Capitol One	UK 0800 952 5267
Citibank	UK 0800 00 55 00
Clydesdale Bank	UK 0845 606 0622
The Co-operative Bank	UK 0845 600 6000
Diners Club	UK 0870 1900 011
	Ireland 0818 300 026
Egg	UK 08451 233 233
First Direct	UK 08456 100 100
GE Capital	UK 0870 125 2515
Goldfish	UK 0800 281 881
Halifax	UK 08456 007 010
Lloyds TSB Bank	UK 0800 096 9779
Marks and Spencer Money UK	0845 900 0900
MBNA Europe	UK 0800 062 062
	Ireland 1800 409 511
Morgan Stanley	UK 0800 02 88 990
National Irish Bank	Ireland 1850 700 221
Nationwide	UK 08457 99 22 22
	UK 08457 30 20 10
Natwest Bank	UK 0870 600 0459
Northern Bank	UK 08705 168654
Royal Bank of Scotland	UK 0126 829 8929
	UK 0870 513 3550
Smile	UK 0845 600 6000
Woolwich	UK 01604 230 230
	UK 0845 0700 360
	0845 677 0009
Yorkshire Bank	UK 08456 060 622
Thomas Cook	UK 0800 622 101

Self-Assessment: Tax Return

Most people do not need to complete self-assessment tax returns as they have normal tax affairs and their employers deduct tax.

However, some people have more complicated tax and need to fill out an annual tax return. This can be done either by completing a paper Self-Assessment Tax Return pack, or can be done online.

A tax return is needed each year if you:
- Work for yourself, either self employed or in partnership
- Are a company director
- Are a minister of religion
- Have income from letting land or property
- Receive income from a trust or settlement e.g. from the estate of a deceased person or if you have taxable foreign income.

If you are an employee or pensioner, you also need to complete a return if:
- You have savings or investments of £10,000 or more (before tax)
- You have an annual income of £100,000 or more.

Once you start employment that requires you to fill a Self-Assessment Tax return, you will need to register yourself as such with the Inland Revenue. This can be done over the phone and is the first step to Self-Assessment. The Newly Self-Employed can register on 08459 15 45 15.

If you are unsure as to whether you need to fill out a Self-Assessment Tax Return, or require assistance filling one out, you can:

Call the Self-Assessment Help line on 0845 9000444
(Open 8am-8pm seven days a week, including bank holidays)

National Insurance Numbers

Do you have your National Insurance number yet?

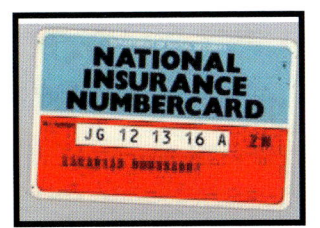

If you do, you must remember to keep it in a safe place as you keep that number for the rest of your life.

If you don't have a National Insurance number you can apply for one, as long as you are 16 or over and have enough evidence to enable the DWP (Benefits Office) to allocate you one.

Your local benefits office will have to interview you about this and you may have to wait some time for an interview.

In the meantime, you may be entitled to an interim payment if you are claiming benefits.

Income support

Income support is a benefit for people with a low income. It isn't paid to people in full-time work (they may be able to get other benefits), or to people who have to be available or actively seeking work (they may be able to get Jobseeker's allowance).

The rules for claiming Income Support, as in all other benefits, are very complicated. There are rules about how much money you can have of your own and still claim Income Support, the limits depend on your own situation. To be 'entitled to Income Support in you own right', you must be 16 years old or over. If you are under 16, someone else may be able to claim on your behalf, such as a parent or guardian.

There are many reasons you may be entitled to Income Support:
- If you are unable to live with your parents.
- If you have a disability or are sick (depending on the extent of the disability, or length of sickness).
- If you are the lone parent of a child or children under 16 years old.

> **If your situation changes it is very important to let your DWP know as you are likely to be held responsible for any money that is overpaid to you.**

INSURANCE

WHAT IS IT? **SHOULD I HAVE IT?** **IS IT WORTH IT?**

Insurance is when you pay sums of money to 'insure' your property, belongings or yourself against something bad happening to them. Something bad has to happen before you can benefit from the money you have paid as Insurance. If something bad did happen, say your house burnt down, as long as your home was Insured, your Insurance company would pay a large sum of money to help you buy a new house.

Assurance is when you are assured of a pay out for example in the case of an endowment.
Nowadays you can insure most things, your car, home, pets even your life!
You pay a certain amount yearly, monthly or weekly to your insurance company and they agree to repair or replace or 'compensate' you by giving you a large sum of money if the thing you insure gets stolen, lost, broken or dies. How much depends on the value of the thing you are insuring, the risk of it getting broken etc and the insurance company you choose.

Insurance is a very good idea to get if you own something that is expensive and you could not afford to replace if it got stolen and it is essential if you own a car as it is illegal to drive without it.

REMEMBER WHEN TAKING OUT INSURANCE.

Shop around. Different companies have different rates and you could save a lot of money.
Make sure you can afford it! Payments can add up and if they want a large yearly payment…can you afford it?
Check and see if it is cheaper to pay yearly. If you can afford the one off payment and it works out cheaper…do it!

CAR INSURANCE

Car insurance is compulsory. This means you have to have it otherwise you are breaking the law if you drive without it. There are usually two choices of car insurance. Third party and fully comprehensive.

Third party, is as it implies, only third parties are insured such as the persons and car of the other vehicle.

Fully comprehensive is what it says. It insures all people and property. Which is best for you is best discussed with your broker or insurance company, as well as other additions such as no claims bonus or legal fees. It could be down to a matter of finance but most companies will now accept staggered payments over the course of the insurance.

HOLIDAY INSURANCE

Holiday insurance is a must. You shouldn't dream of going without it. Anybody planning to do anything more energetic than swim in the hotel pool or dance in nightclubs should think about taking out extra cover. Bear in mind that even relatively common holiday pursuits such as riding a motorbike or horse are considered as 'dangerous' activities by some insurers.

When you opt for dangerous sports-cover, make sure that your particular activity is included: some policies will cover parachuting but not bungee jumping, for example, some may frown on white-water rafting but not pot-holing. There are no rules. It is a matter of phoning individual insurers and asking whether your chosen sport is covered.

If you have a problem with an insurance company always try and sort it out with them

first, keep copies of all correspondence, numbers and times of contact). If this fails and the company is regulated by the Financial Services Authority, ring them on help-line:
0845 606 1234.
For travel insurance problems you should contact the Ombudsman.
0845 080 1800.
Extended warranties on electrical goods should be reported to the Department of Trade and Industries…
020 7215 5417

What To Do If It All Goes Wrong

Situation 1: Your flight is delayed
If the flight is delayed more than five hours you are entitled to meals, two free phone calls and a full refund! More information about this can be found at www.auc.org.uk or you can call 020 7240 6061

Situation 2: My luggage is missing
- If you have insurance you need to call your insurance company or check any documents you have been given when you got the insurance. Check if it covers luggage going missing.
- Keep the barcode receipts you are given when you board your luggage onto the plane
- Report it immediately to your airline

Situation 3: Your hotel room is more like a hellhole
- Keep detailed records of your complaints (see our complaints section).
- Ask for more suitable accommodation.
- If you are denied make sure you take photographs or even better video evidence of the situation.
- Ask other holidaymakers if they are in the same situation and record what they say 'this is taking a statement'.
- As soon as you get home write to your travel agent they should reply to your complaint in 28 days.

If Things go Wrong with a Holiday Booking
Take Immediate Action
Make your complaint to the companies representative with all the evidence relating to your booking and the brochure that features details of what you were promised.

1. **Keep a Record** Take notes and photographs of what you are complaining about and keep receipts of any extras you have been forced to pay for as a result (make sure you keep a copy of all photographs and receipts). If others in your party feel the same way, take their names and addresses and if possible a short statement. Collective action is always more effective.

2. **Contact the tour or flight operator** Write to both tour operator and travel agent on your return (check the small print on the brochure as there may be a time limit for complaints). Keep a copy of everything you send.

3. **Taking it further** If after two letters to the operator or agent you are still not satisfied, take your complaint to the higher body.

Association of British Travel Agents (ABTA)

55 Newman Street, London, W1P 4AH .

Association of Independent Tour Operators (AITO)

133a St Margaret's Road, Twickenham, Middlesex, TW1 1RG.

The Air Transport Users Council will provide information and guidance if your complaint is against an airline. Send a letter that clearly lays out your case and send to; AUC 5th floor, Kingsway House, London, WCB 6QX

4. **Trading Standards Office** If you are unhappy with the results of your complaint, contact your local trading standards office. They deal with holiday and travel incidents that contravene the new E.C directive on package travel, package holiday and package tours.

The directive states that the brochure now forms part of the contract and that all details given therein are binding.

Travel companies are now no longer allowed to add disclaimers for responsibility for the accuracy of content.

5. **Arbitration or small claims court** Your final recourse is to choose between ABTA's arbitration scheme which can take about three months or to seek compensation through the small claims court, but can take up to nine months. Bearing in mind, you are banned from pursuing both courses and that the result of any hearing is final and binding on both parties.

PAINTING & DECORATING TIPS

DOING IT YOURSELF

… Even moving into gran's caravan for a while? Everyone likes a comfortable and easy to keep clean space to live in. Decorating or attempting to do it yourself will of course depend on your living arrangements. If you're sharing maybe you want to spruce up your room. Or are you renting for now but just can't stand the last tenant's like for floral? Or maybe you're thinking about buying but have no funds available now to modernise your palace.

Included in this chapter are a few basic DIY tips to get you going.   If DIY is something you haven't had time for in the past, give it a go, it won't take long for you to get the bug especially if you develop the eye for a bargain.

BUDGETING

-Keep your eye out for car boot sales, which are great for bargains, and for finding those items you have been wanting for.

-In sales you can also find household items at great prices

-Trying to make the most of what you already have. This can be a great challenge but you would be amazed at how you can transform things if only you know how, so do some research and don't be afraid to experiment. In a different colour, in a different place how else could it look?

-There are more and more manufactured household shops that create modern, likeable furniture and goods at great affordable prices. Ikea for example offers cheap easy to construct furniture and complete with an idiots guide, perfect.

It's impossible to budget effectively and get absolutely everything you need for your new place. It takes time, which is all in the fun of setting up on your own, and having it exactly how you want it.

It is sensible to spend most from your budget on items with the greatest use and value.

A reliable fridge and cooker for example are important as is a washing machine and if you would like to sleep; a good bed. I suppose spending your time at the local launderette and burger joint would get you by for a while but spending money and time now, if you can, will save you money and time later.

PREPARING A ROOM

Take down all fixtures and fittings in the room. This saves a lot of time trying to paint round them neatly, which can, in the long, end up messy. For electrical fittings make sure you turn off al the power first before attempting to undo or remove them.

Do not turn the power back on until the work is finished. Clear all furniture from the room. Anything you can't move put it in the center of the room and use dust-sheets to cover so they do not accidentally get paint etc on them.

PREPARING WOODWORK

If the woodwork you wish to paint is already painted but the paint is cracked and worn you will need to strip it off. If the wood you wish to paint is already painted and in good condition there is no need to strip it and you can use the existing paint as a good base for the new paint. Rub down the surface of the woodwork with some medium grade sandpaper, (this can be obtained from any D.I.Y. store).

You may still need to strip paint where it is so thick it causes your windows or doors to jam.

PREPARING WALLS AND CEILINGS

Firstly, make sure you hack off all the loose and excess plaster. Use plenty of sugar soap and clean water to wash down all wooden surfaces and allow them to dry before painting.

Be careful around electrical fittings and protect them from water.

Fill holes with plaster filler or a deep-repair cellulose filler, 9both may be obtained from any D.I.Y. store).

Some cracks may need to be filled in a couple of stages so check the instructions before using either product. The cellulose filler is suitable for small holes and cracks. Use a flexible knife to force the filler into the hole. If you can't get a smooth finish with the knife simply leave the filler slightly overflowing from the hole, leave to dry and then rub it smooth with dry sandpaper.

PAINTING WALLS AND CEILINGS

Make sure you have enough time to do this in one go! If you stop and start you will get a line where the paint has dried unevenly. Bare plaster needs to be prepared first by painting with a diluted coat of emulsion paint then left to dry before painting the colours of your choice. This is known as 'priming'. You need to prime the surface that has been painted previously.

A lick of paint can do wonderful things. If you have any old paint left, strain it through a pair of nylon tights to remove lumps.

If you have used your best or last brush to paint gloss but have no turpentine left to clean the brush...simply wrap the bristles with cling film to avoid the brush from hardening.

Try painting everything white. When starting completely from scratch it can be cheaper and easier to do it this way. It shows all the flaws that need to be filled and gives you a blank canvass to work with.

PREPARATION: BRUSHES

Investing in a good set of brushes is essential and though it may cost you a bit more than the cheaper alternative, as long as you take good care of them you will save in the long run. Using cheap brushes can lead to bristles coming off when you are painting and making a mess of whatever you are painting. Also, they will need replacing very often.

To clean brushes suspend them in a jar, (one for each brush), using a nail and a piece of string. Fill the jar regularly with cleaning solution which should also be changed regularly. To store clean brushes use an elastic band to hold the bristles together while they dry. This will keep their shape so there are no stray bristles.

Once the brush is dry store it in a sealed polythene bag which will stop them getting dusty and store flat so the brush keeps its shape.

MASKING PAINTWORK

Stick strips of masking tape around the edges of the glass panes when painting door and window frames. This will save a lot of time later in cleaning up. If you accidentally paint on the glass it will now go on the tape instead. Remove the tape as soon as the paint is dry or it will be harder to get off later on.

LEFT OVER PAINT

Don't leave left over paint in the tin it originally came in or it will dry up. Keep the left over paint stored in jars that are small enough to be filled to the top with left over paint. If there is no air left in the jar when the lid is screwed on tightly it should keep it for use at a later date.

OLD PAINT   If you have any old paint…go check now!

If it has a brown liquid on the top just stir it…don't throw it away. This is usual if paint has been left for some time. If a skin has formed on the top, simply cut around the skin with scissors and strain the paint.

Obviously not using the type of strainer that will be later used with food or beverages such as a colander or tea strainer).

If you have an emulsion paint that is in a can that has gone rusty on the inside, carefully remove the paint not affected and throw the rest away.

PAINT

PRIMER

This seals a surface to prevent subsequent layers of paint sinking and disappearing. Primers are made for wood, metal and plaster, while universal primers are designed to suit all three surfaces.

UNDERCOAT

A paint formulated to obliterate the previous colour and give body to the next coating. Some gloss paints are self-undercoating.

GLOSS

Gloss paint, as it implies, is a shiny finish and is harder than most other finishes. It is ideal for doors and windows. All surfaces must have a primer and undercoat first. You only need to wipe with a soapy cloth to keep it looking new.

EMULSION

Mostly used for walls and ceilings. As it is water-based emulsion is quick-drying, easy to use (and to rinse out of brushes) and reasonably odourless. It is not suitable for wood since it may cause the grain to rise. Emulsions come as liquid, thixotropic or non-drip.

Removing Wallpaper: Vinyl/Easy Strip Wallpaper

There are a lot of wallpapers that leave the bottom layer intact but you can strip the top layer off by loosening a corner at the bottom and pulling away like in the diagram below. Simply pull the decorative layer off like the diagram above. You can paper over the bottom layer left behind but cannot paint over it. If you want to paint over it you will need to soak the paper using a sponge and warm water mixed with washing up liquid and strip it off using a scraper.

Washable Wallpaper

To remove washable wallpaper you will need to use a serrated edge scraper or course grade of glass paper (though this might get clogged up quickly). Scrape the surface and then soak it with warm water and washing up liquid using a sponge.

Hessian Wallpaper

This is usually used to cover up problems with plaster beneath it so be very careful when removing it. Check areas of the wall before stripping off. If the wall appears in a bad condition don't remove.

Lincruster

This is really hard to remove as it is stuck down with a very strong adhesive. Use hot water and a scraper to carefully remove the sheets without taking any plaster with it. If there is any adhesive left, repeat the process.

Cork Wall Tiles/Expanded Polystyrene Tiles

Force the tiles away from the wall using a flexible scraper then use a hot-air stripper or blowlamp to remove the adhesive left on the wall but BE CAREFUL.

Stripping Ceilings

For this you will need a steam stripper machine. Before you use it make sure you have read the instructions thoroughly as there is a risk of burning. You will need to put water into the stripper and turn it on. Put the stripper with the big flat surface flat on the ceiling like in the image below. When you pull the handle the steam should come out and start to soak the paper so it comes away from the wall (use a scraper to help the paper away from the wall but don't be too forceful). It is advisable not to do this alone as it is dangerous not to mention the arm ache you get!

PREVENTING DAMP AND MOULD

A problem that arises very frequently especially in flats, is dampness and mould. Whilst not being life threatening, it can be a real health hazard, but with very little effort can be cured.

Damp causes mould on walls and furniture, mites that can cause respiratory diseases and rotting of window frames and skirting boards.

Damp can be caused by leaking pipes, rain leaking into the house or water rising up from the ground as the house has been built on ground without proper drains.

If your house is new it may have damp just because the plaster that the house is made of is still a little wet. To solve this you can hire a dehumidifier or heat the house.

Another method would be to open every window in the house to create a through draught.

However if it is none of the above reasons it is probably caused by 'Condensation'. This is basically a scaled down version of rain. There is water in the air (there is always water in the air even if you can't see it) that settles on surfaces if they are cold making them wet/damp.

To avoid condensation:

- Cover pans when boiling liquid.
- Do not leave kettles boiling
- Dry washing outdoors if possible or dry in the bathroom with the window open and a fan on
- Make sure if you have a tumble dryer its vent is outside and if it is not buy a DIY kit to ensure your dryer does vent outside
- Keep windows open a small amount when you are in the room
- Use extractor fans if your house has them
- Use a humidistat-controlled electric fan. This will turn on if the air has too much moisture in it that could cause condensation
- Do not overfill cupboards and wardrobes and make sure there is a ventilation hole in them to let air in and out so moisture doesn't get trapped in one place

- Insulate your loft
- Get cavity wall insulation (contact a building inspector first)
- Get double glazed windows
- In cold weather leave the heating on a small amount even if there is no one home

You should not:
- Block permanent ventilators
- Block chimneys
- Draughtproof rooms that have condensation or mould
- Draughtproof any rooms that have a cooker or fire of any kind

Mould

To get rid of mould you will need to wipe it off walls and window frames with a fungicidal wash that you can buy from your local DIY store. Make sure you get one with a Health and Safety Executive Approval Number and READ THE INSTRUCTIONS. Dry clean any clothes that have mould and shampoo any carpets that have mould. You should then paint any surfaces that had mould on them with a fungicidal paint that you can also buy from your local DIY store.
Domestos or any other bleach is a very good substitute for over-priced fungicides.
DO NOT: Brush or vacuum mould it will cause more of it to be released into the air which causes respiratory problems
DO NOT: Paint over or wallpaper over fungicidal paint as this stops it working.

Useful contacts if you need more help or information about damp and mould:

Home Energy Efficiency Scheme: 0800 072 0150
Energy Savings Trust – 0345 277 200
Department of the Environment, Transport and the Regions– 0870 1226 236)
'Tackling Condensation' a book that can help – BRE – 01923 664444 – 01923 664664

Electrical Problems in the Home

You should have a box of switches and fuses somewhere in your house, if you don't you will need to seek professional help as your house may need rewiring. If you do not know where your fuse box is you need to find out! This box controls all the electrical circuits in your house (the plugs, lights etc) and should have switches to turn them off/on. It is sometimes called a Consumer Unit.

Fuses

Fuses are there basically there to stop your TV, computer, light bulbs etc from blowing up if there is a surge in power. Instead of the TV blowing up for example if too much power is going through your house, the fuse will blow itself up.

Miniature Circuit Breakers and Residual Current Devices

The fuses in your fuse box don't normally need to be replaced instead the Miniature Circuit Breakers or Residual Current Device in your fuse box will automatically turn off the switch for that circuit so you will just have to flip it back to on again.

What to Do If The Lights/ Electricity Goes Off

Don't panic! Go to your fuse box and check and see if the switches are on. If one of them is switched off simply flip the switch back to on again and the electricity should come back on. If the switch keeps flipping off unplug an appliance and try again. When it comes on again it might be that the appliance you unplugged was faulty so get it checked out. If it is the lights that won't come back on check with neighbours, it may be a power cut in which case you will just have to wait it out. Light candles if it is dark but be very careful not to leave them unattended.

What to Do if an Appliance is Faulty Unplug the appliance. If you suspect an appliance is faulty carefully check that the wires connecting it have not been cut or broken. Check that water has not leaked or spilled onto the appliance. If this is the case take the appliance to be repaired.

Ask how much it will cost first and then if it is cheaper to replace you can replace it. If you have insurance on the item call your insurance company and they should compensate you. If none of these things applies to you then check the plug using the instructions below.

Circuit fault

If a circuit fails you need to turn off all lights or disconnect all appliances that are on that circuit. Then you should turn off the power at the main switch which will be in your consumer unit. You need to replace the fuse 12

Always remember to be careful when using electrical appliances

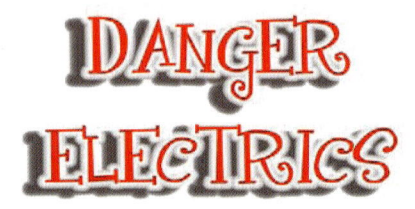

DANGER ELECTRICS

Your life could be at risk. You must take precautions and not take risks or major repairs. Leave them to the professionals.

Working safely

Before beginning any kind or electrical work, you must always take the following safety precautions.

- Switch off the main power at the consumer unit (fuse box)
- Isolate the circuit you plan to work on by removing the circuit fuse and putting it in your pocket. Or switch off and lock the relevant circuit breaker. If you can't lock it, tape the switch in the off position, and attach a very clear note to the unit stating that you are working on the circuit
- Check the circuit is dead with a plug in socket tester or, in the case of a lighting circuit, a voltage tester

When you have finished, replace the fuse/circuit breaker and turn the main power switch on again. Never restore power until the faceplates and covers of all accessories have been fitted.

There are a lot of talented people in the world but without dedication they are nothing.

Wiring safety and materials

Electricity is profoundly deadly, so safety is the by-word when it comes to carrying out any electrical work in the home. The following pages describe some of the most useful repairs and improvements you can make to a domestic wiring system, from connecting up a plug to making a simple extension to a lighting circuit, but it is most important that you use only the correct materials and tools when carrying out this work, and have in mind the vital common-sense do's and don'ts noted in the box below.

Do's and don'ts

- Don't attempt electrical work unless you know what you are doing and are confident you can carry it out safely
- Do turn off the main system on/off switch before starting any wiring work
- Don't touch any electrical fitting or appliance with wet hands, and never take a portable appliance into the bathroom on an extension lead
- Do unplug appliances before attempting to inspect or repair them
- Don't omit earth connections when wiring appliances
- Do double-check connections

NB: Diagram of plug and fuses

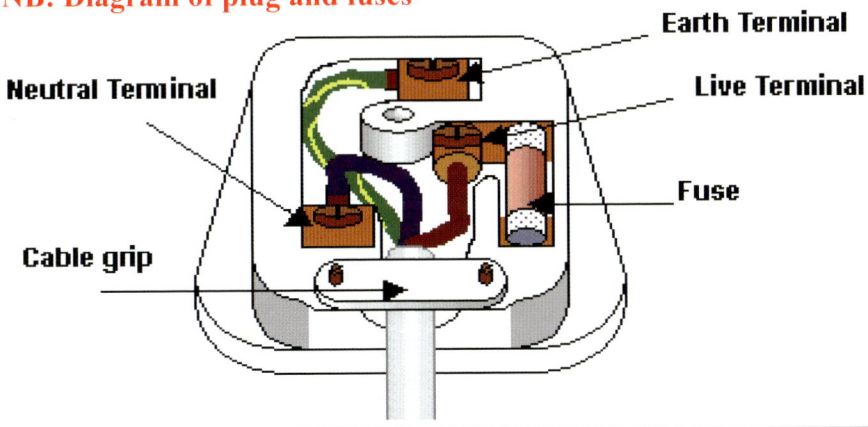

Standard wire colours for plugs

	Live	Neutral	Earth
United Kingdom	Red	Black	Green

SIMPLE WIRING TASKS

Two of the most basic wiring tasks that are undertaken about the home are fitting a new plug and wiring up a pendent light fitting. Although simple tasks, whenever dealing with electricity, make sure to use the right materials and make all connections firm and secure. With post terminals, a screw secures the core. With stud terminals, the core is held by a washer.

Wiring a Plug

The plug is the all-important link between an electrical appliance and the mains and must be wired up correctly. The cores must be linked securely to the terminals – brown to live (the fused terminal), blue neutral and green-yellow to earth – and the cord grid securely engaged to prevent tension on the cores. The plug must always be in good condition; it is all too easy to touch live parts as the plug is handled, with potentially fatal results. Always fit the right fuse: a red 3-amp for appliances up to 690 watts, a brown 13-amp fuse otherwise.

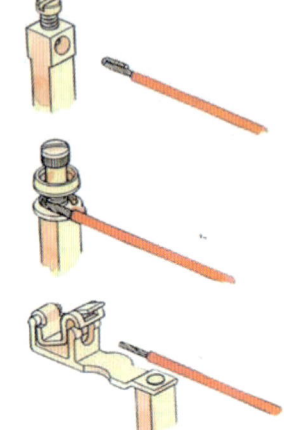

!!!!! BEWARE THE DODGY ELCTRICIAN!!!!!

Only employ electricians that are NICEIC approved. You can find these electricians on the NICEIC website: www.niceic.org.uk or by calling them on 020 7564 23 20 or look in your yellow pages. If any work is done on your house by one of these electricians they should show you a certificate to prove that they are qualified to do such work to the correct standard. If they do not show you one when the work is completed ask to see it. If they do not have one or you suspect the work is shoddy report it to the NICEIC and DO NOT PAY THE ACCOUNT.

If you suspect any electrics in your house is faulty or dangerous, report it to the NICEIC.

Plumbing Emergencies

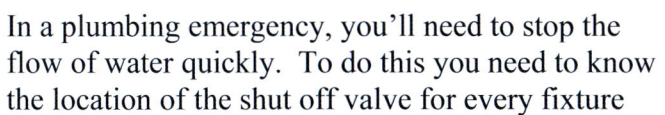

In a plumbing emergency, you'll need to stop the flow of water quickly. To do this you need to know the location of the shut off valve for every fixture and fitting as well as the main shut off valve for the house, and how they operate. This is commonly known as a stopcock.

The council owns and maintains a stopcock, controlling the water supply to each property. This is generally located in the same box as the water meter and is located just beyond the front boundary in the footpath area.

To comply with the Building Industry Act and Water Supply Bylaw each property should also have a stopcock owned by and operated by the property owner, located within the private property.

If the emergency involves a specific fixture or appliance, first look for its shut off valve and turn it clockwise to shut off the water.

The valve is usually located underneath a fixture such as a sink or toilet, or behind an appliance, such as a clothes washer, at the point where the water supply pipe/s connects to it.

If the problem is not with a particular fixture or appliance, or there is no shutoff valve for the fixture or appliance, use the main shutoff valve to turn off the water supply to the entire house.

A good tip is to keep a spanner or wrench very near, to help you turn off the stopcock as soon as possible, meaning you don't have to search for one as water is cascading down the stairs.

If the main shutoff valve itself is defective and needs to be repaired call your water company; they can send someone out with the special tools needed to shut off the water supply before it reaches the appliance's valve.

A leaking or broken pipe

Turn off the main shutoff valve to prevent water damage.
Make temporary repairs to stop the leak.
The pipe will have to be replaced as soon as possible.

A blocked sink

Turn off any tap or appliance such as a dish washer that drains into the sink.
Unclog the sink using a plunger – see below.

DON'T use a chemical drain cleaner if the blockage is total.
Every so often pour bleach into the sink and leave overnight to prevent blockages.
When you have extra boiled water such as a saucepan after cooking or a boiled kettle pour this down the sink to prevent grease and muck building up.

Cleaning drains with a plunger

The plunger is a good drain-clearing tool but it often fails to work because it is used incorrectly. Don't make the mistake of pumping up and down two or three times expecting water to whoosh down the drain. No great expertise is needed just follow these guidelines:
1) Choose a plunger with a suction cup large enough to cover the drain completely.
2) Fill the clogged sink with enough water to cover the plunger cup.
3) Coat the rim of the plunger with petroleum jelly to ensure a tight seal.
4) Block off all the other outlets (the overflow, second drain in a double sink, adjacent fixtures with wet rags.
5) Insert the plunger into the water at an angle so no air remains trapped under it.
6) Use fifteen to twenty forceful strokes, holding the plunger upright and pumping vigorously.
7) Repeat the plunging two or three times before giving up.

Using chemical drain cleaners

Through routine use of chemical drain cleaners to prevent clogs, you may eventually damage your pipes. But they can be useful. If water is draining slowly but plunging has failed to solve the problem a drain cleaner may be helpful. When using these chemicals do so with caution and in a well ventilated room. Be sure to take these precautions:
1) Never use a plunger if chemicals are present as they risk splashing you.
2) Wear gloves to prevent burning or irritation of the skin
3) Don't use a chemical cleaner if the blockage is total
4) Never use a chemical cleaner in a garbage disposal
5) Read labels and match the type of cleaners with the type of blockage. (Alkalis cut grease; acids dissolve soap and hair.)

Replacing a tap washer

One of the most common faults and easily replaceable things to do and can save you considerable amounts of money is to replace tap washer.
Firstly turn the water off at the stop cock!!
- A) Using a set of pliers remove the head of the tap. Don't dismantle the shroud (covering)
- B) Take of the washer
- C) Put a new washer into place and reassemble the tap using appliers.

Troubleshooting toilet problems: Running toilet

Check for:	Remedies:
<ul><li>Float arm not rising high enough</li><li>Water filled float boat</li><li>Tank stopper not seating properly</li><li>Corroded flush valve seal</li><li>Cracked overflow tube</li><li>Ball cock doesn't shut off</li></ul>	<ul><li>Bend float arm down or away from tank wall</li><li>Replace the ball</li><li>Adjust stopper guide rod and lift wires or chain. Replace defective stopper</li><li>Scour valve seat or replace</li><li>Replace tube or install new flush valve assembly</li><li>Oil trip level, replace faulty washers or put in a new ball cock assembly.</li></ul>

Noisy toilet

Check for:	Remedies:
<ul><li>Restricted water flow</li><li>Defective ball cock assembly</li></ul>	<ul><li>Adjust the shutoff valve first</li><li>Oil the trip lever or replace the ball cock washers.</li><li>Replace the entire ball cock assembly</li><li>CAUTION: First turn off the water at the water at the fixture shutoff valve. Then flush the toilet.</li></ul>

6 GUARANTEED WAYS NOT ONLY TO MAKE YOUR LIFE BETTER.... BUT ALSO PROLONG IT!!

- **Cut Salt from your diet**

- **Banish sugar**

- **Drink a minimum of 8 pints of water a day**

- **Breath correctly**

- **Eat the right foods**

- **Stop smoking**

These points are so important that you could do no better for your general health and well-being than to copy this and frame it, display it in a prominent position. You couldn't help a friend more than to give them a copy.

1. Salt

Salt is a killer it contributes to many heart problems and deaths, there is enough salt in the food you eat during the course of a day, so you don't need to add anymore!!

2. Sugar

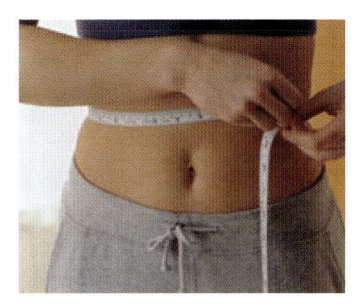

Probably the biggest fraud food of them all! It adds no protein and no worthwhile benefits to anyone. If you put three spoons of sugar in your tea or coffee, try putting in 2 ½ for a month then 2 for the next month and so on, till eventually you can do away with it all. I promise you after 4 or 5 months, put 3 spoonfuls of sugar in your beverage and you will be revolted by the taste. After 6 months you won't experience the highs and lows with your blood count that you have been used to. You will save ££ in your pocket and pounds on your hips!!

3. Water

Drinking water is obviously a must, before all the sweet drinks and caffeine drinks; there was only one choice, <u>WATER</u>. 'Corporation pop' as it used to be known, is more satisfying and more beneficial to the body than any drink you can think of. It has no calories, no added E numbers and no sugars. Just pure water. But don't wait until you are thirsty though, that's the body's way of telling you you're dehydrating. Drink at least 2 litres to feel the most benefit and do the most good. It will help to flush out of your system all the toxins and poisons in your body.

4. Breathing

Breathing is the most natural thing we do, but very few people breathe correctly. You should inhale through the nose, and exhale through the mouth.

The greatest exercise you can do is to:
1. Lie down on the floor or the bed,
2. Inhale through the nose as much as you can right down to your stomach area. Extending the stomach as if you were pregnant.
3. Hold for 4 to 5 seconds and exhale slowly through the mouth.

Do this for 10 minutes at least daily. The benefits you will find are enormous. It will make feel more relaxed and tranquil as well as enriching the blood supply to your heart.

5. Food

Food and the right type of food, as Martina Navratilova says is more important then exercise. Given the choice for a healthy life style, she would plump for a healthy food diet every time. Try and eat less processed foods eat more vegetables and fruit, the more you eat things that grow, and less of the ones that roam on 4 legs the better. Food that is natural is so much better for you. Wholemeal products are so much tastier than their cardboard tasting counterparts. Just take the time to look at the number of additives you find in the tins and packets in the cupboards of your kitchen. Look them up and it will frighten you.

6. Smoking

Smoking, knowing the facts that we do now, is nothing short of criminal! I would recommend that every smoker visit their local NHS hospital and see the number of people on ventilators, other with oxygen trailers and others At the very least bed bound. It would lower the number of people smoking considerably. But its not only that, its stupid, can you imagine a Alien landing on earth and asking what people are doing with bits of paper in their mouth and someone explaining that it is a weed wrapped in paper that you set fire to and not only costs a lot of money but eventually almost certainly will kill you, I'd think they would be on the first flight home! The number of ailments associated with smoking would cover another hundred pages in this book. To improve your health at a stroke, give up now; you will never do another thing that can improve the quality of your life than this on decision.

Body Maintenance

Being on your own for the first time may leave you feeling depressed and even unwanted. The temptation may be to comfort eat.

This in turn may result in loading on the pounds…which in turn adds to the already felt misery!

I liken the human body to a car. The difference is that if you leave a car stationary in the garage but also keep pumping petrol into the tank…the petrol will, obviously, overflow and flood the floor. If you fail to service your car, for example never put essential oils in the engine, pretty soon the engine will seize up.

In the case of a human body, keep pumping food into it without burning it off the extra calories have to go somewhere and that is when those unwanted inches start to appear.

Food, unlike petrol, does not have a tank to overflow from. Therefore the body *has* to grow to retain the extra intake.

Also if you fail to use the correct oils and fluids in a car the valves and workings cease to function. This is exactly the same for the body. Eating the wrong type of food which lacks the necessary nutrients or vitamins leads to all types of illnesses including heart problems.

It may look good on the plate but will it look good on your hips?

You need to exercise intensively for 5-6 hours in order to lose 1 lb of fat, but it is much easier to put less sugar in your beverage or less butter on your toast.
If you lose ½ lb of fat a week in a year you will have lost 2 stone.

Nothing tastes as good, as being slim feels.

10 Top Eating Tips

1. **Eat regular meals.** Never miss a meal.
2. **Avoid** all sugar and refined foods.
3. **Avoid** alcohol.
4. **Eat something raw** before each meal, a carrot or a salad.
5. **Cut out saturated fats.** Choose olive oil. Eating less saturated fat will also help you lose weight. Have low fat skimmed milk and yogurt. Grill, steam or oven bake food and drain all fat.
6. **Don't have artificial sweeteners-** they may not have all the calories but they maintain a sweet tooth.
7. **Eat more** than two pieces of fruit a day.
8. **Never** eat starchy carbohydrates on their own.
9. **Eat protein with a high biological value (BV) at each meal.** Foods with a BV of more than 75 help balance glucose. They are eggs, cheese, milk, fish, beef, chicken and Soya.
10. Chew food properly and make sure that you eat slowly.

Smoking

Just imagine the scene. A Martian arrives on Earth and sees someone smoking. (This part of his advanced research he hadn't done because he couldn't understand someone putting a piece of burning paper in his or her mouth) But then it was explained to him what this piece of fire did to people.

Namely, it could:

- give you emphysema and various chest and lung problems
- bring on heart attacks
- be responsible for a multitude of health problems
- give you bad breath
- curtail your sex life
- ruin your clothes
-

And not only that, but it would also cost an absolute fortune and the result was that it would eventually kill you.

Our Martian would say, 'You're having a laugh!' because the research in this area had led him to watch *Extras* with Ricky Gervais.

There isn't one reason for smoking. I have never heard anyone make a case for smoking, not even the tobacco companies, with their vast sums of money. If they could think of one good reason for smoking, however tenuous, you can be sure that by now they would have informed you and would be advertising the fact.

I don't want to preach to you - you've probably been inundated with advice and terrible premonitions from friends, family etc.

But make no mistake - it will kill you.

If you need any proof, visit your local hospital and go in to the chest wards. There you will see people with oxygen masks walking about with the aid of a Zimmer frames, and each one of them clutching an inhaler.

Smoking may not only lead to serious health problems, such as heart disease, strokes and lung and throat cancer to name but a few. It can also affect your body in different ways, affecting the way you look and feel about yourself.

If you, like many others, want to give up, but just never seem to get around to it, it is worth remembering that the sooner you give up, the sooner your body will start recovering from the harm you've done to it, for example, within a week of stopping smoking you will see a difference in your appearance.

For other health problems, however, it can take much, much longer to reduce your risk, so the sooner you quit, the better!

BOYS	GIRLS
There is a valve inside your penis that traps the blood inside in order to allow for you to get an erection. However, each cigarette you smoke causes that valve to become damaged. That's why 120,000 men who smoke can no longer get an erection at all. So what would you rather have? A cigarette or an erection?	The chemicals transferred through your body from a cigarette starve your hair and skin of oxygen, with one cigarette starving your skin of oxygen for over an hour. This abuse of your hair makes it dull, lifeless and brittle which no conditioner can repair, and your skin will also become dull, grey and thin. So what would you rather have? A cigarette or healthy, attractive hair and skin?

How I gave up

One way of giving up, and which I found particularly useful, was not say that I was giving up, but that I stopped and would start smoking again next Wednesday at 3 o' clock. When 3 o'clock Wednesday came, I would say that I would start smoking again on Tuesday at 9 0'clock. And so on and so forth.

Remember that those first three weeks are critical.

After that, the pain, suffering and withdrawal symptoms progressively get easier, but you will probably never lose your addiction.

After a few months, however, the benefits in your mind start to outweigh your desire for tobacco.

The additional help I had was that it coincided with my annual holiday, and lying on a sun lounger on the beach it occurred to me that if I gave up smoking I could do this three times a year with the money I saved. However if I kept smoking I'd be stuck in windswept, rainy England, suffering from the subsequent health problems linked to smoking and gradually killing myself.

The Choice Is Yours

Life   Death

ALCOHOL

YOU CAN'T CALCULATE YOUR ALCOHOL LIMIT.

The legal limit for driving is 80mg of alcohol per 100ml of blood. There is no fail-safe guide to how much you can drink to stay under this limit. The amount and type of alcoholic drink, your weight, your height and metabolism will all play their part.

It is a myth that you can calculate the amount of alcohol you are drinking in this way, in fact the alcohol content of beers, wines and spirits varies so greatly that to rely on guesswork like this is risking your license and your life.

Several factors determine the level of alcohol in your blood:

1. Sex
2. Weight
3. Metabolism
4. Type and quantity of drink
5. Age

Any alcohol, **even a small drink,** will impair driving ability.

The only safe course is not to drink and drive!

Risks

Excessive consumption of alcohol on a regular and sustained basis has been linked to high blood pressure, strokes, heart disease, birth defects, osteoporosis and certain cancers. Among drinkers that smoke these risks are increased.

Drinking alcohol in moderation however, can convey some health benefits due to the level of antioxidants it contains, particularly in red wine and to a far lesser degree in dark brown beers.

The antioxidants in red wine are called polyphenols, which help counter the impact of oxidative stress and probably confer a protective role against cancer and heart disease. However, this is only effective when keeping to the recommended levels of alcohol consumption per week. Binge sessions should be avoided – alcohol intake should be spread over the whole week.

There are sexual risks associated with drinking. Drinking can put you into a state where you are not fully aware of your actions and may corrupt your decision-making skills. A lot of rape related crime is linked to alcohol.
You are putting yourself at risk from sexually transmitted diseases if you have unprotected sex whilst under the influence.
Drinking alcohol also causes sexual difficulties in men such as temporary impotence.

Furthermore drinking alcohol excessively can cause alcohol poisoning, leading to coma and even death.

Consequences

If you are found to be over the legal alcohol limit whilst in charge of a vehicle (this means even sitting in your car not necessarily driving it) you can face fines of up to £5000 and/or a jail sentence of up to 6 months and almost certainly a twelve month ban from driving. Of course if you cause or are involved in an accident whilst under the influence the terms are far more serious. Should you run someone over, crash in to them or are in anyway linked to the cause of their death the current sentence is up to 14 years in prison.

Again………The **only** safe course is not to drink and drive!

Some advice when drinking

- Always try and eat something either before or whilst you are drinking
- If you have drunk large quantities of alcohol, drink plenty of water afterwards. This will counteract dehydration.
- Rather than drink coffee the morning after a drinking session, a breakfast consisting of carbohydrates (cereal and toast), a glass of fresh fruit juice and a cup of green tea should bring your blood sugar level up to an acceptable level and help you rehydrate your body.
- Never, ever drink when taking any form of medication/illegal drugs/playing sports/working at height or working machinery

Units

A unit of alcohol is defined as follows:

- 250ml (1/2 pint) of ordinary strength beer/lager
- one glass (125ml/4 fl oz) of wine
- one pub measure of sherry/vermouth (31.25ml/1.5 fl oz)
- one pub measure of spirits (31.25ml/1.5 fl oz)

It is advised by the British government not to exceed the following units per week at the risk of poor health:

Women: no more than 14
Men: no more than 21

The current unit consumption known as a binge drinking session is assumed to be the following amount of units in one drinking session:

Women: 6 or more
Men: 8 or more

DRUGS

Some drugs are called 'Prescription drugs'. These are the legal type so long as a doctor prescribes them to you. Some drugs you can buy without having a prescription (signed piece of paper by a doctor saying you can buy them). Paracetamol is a drug you can buy from chemists such as Boots or Superdrug without a prescription. These are legal to as long as you take them yourself and do not give them to other people without their permission. Drugs such as these are not used for what is known as recreational use. This is to get a certain sensation that is sometimes pleasant or sometimes used to avoid personal feelings and causes a lack of sensation. These drugs are divided into three classes regarding the law but all are harmful and potentially fatal. Giving any drug even a paracetamol to someone without permission is illegal.

If you are caught in possession of a Class C drug you could be put in prison for up to 2 years and fined. This increases to up to 7 years in prison and a fine if you are caught in possession of a Class A drug.

If you are caught selling drugs however the punishments are even more severe. For having the intention to supply a Class C drug you could face up to 5 years in prison and a fine, for Class B up to 14 years in prison and a fine and if you have the intent to supply a Class A drug you could be fined and put in prison for life! These sentences can be passed if you are caught in possession of drugs as it looks like you have the intent to supply and even if you are just holding the drugs for someone else it can look like this so best bet is to say no to holding drugs even just for a second.

Class A drugs currently include: Magic Mushrooms (when prepared for use), Speed/Amphetamines (when prepared for injection), Heroin, Acid (LSD), Cocaine and Crack, Ecstacy and Methadone.

Class B drugs are: Speed/Amphetamines

Class C drugs are: Rohypnol, Steroids, Tranquilizers, Sleeping Pills, Valium, Temazepam, GHB and cannabis.

SOLVENT ABUSE

There is presently no categorisation for solvents, as such, but it is illegal to sell or give them to anyone under the age of 18. This is a safeguard against younger people attempting to sniff or inhale them. Glue, paint, gases, such as butane, aerosols, and even tip-ex are common items utilised for abuse. The sensations of solvent abuse are dizziness, depression, loss of memory. It can also cause heart failure, where your heart quite literally stops working. It can also instantaneously kill by freezing your airways causing suffocation. Solvent abuse can and often will cause liver and kidney failure.
Solvents tend to leave you with a headache, which can be very severe. Many people dabble with solvent abuse due to peer pressure or to seek distraction from their day-to-day problems. Unfortunately, solvent abuse can soon become addictive and the end result can have tragic consequences.

All medicines are drugs but not all drugs are medicines

TOBACCO

The addictive drug in tobacco is called Nicotine and it can affect different people in different ways. For some people it can become addictive straight away whereas for some it takes a while before they feel addicted to Nicotine. The only way to tell for sure if you are addicted to Nicotine is to quit. Thinking you can quit if you tried is the first symptom of addiction.

Nicotine is harmful as it increases the pulse rate and raises blood pressure. However it is not the only harmful chemical in tobacco. There are up to 4000 chemicals in cigarette smoke that harm the body as well as the harm involved in ingesting smoke. Tobacco is commonly smoked in cigarettes which are bought ready rolled or it can be rolled into a cigarette using paper sometimes called skins as it contains the tobacco.

Nicotine can cause new users to feel dizzy and sick but can sometimes cause a feeling of relaxation. This feeling of relaxation when it ends can cause severe irritation and depression. Smoking causes coughs, chest and breathing problems, bad breath, stained teeth, ulcers, wrinkles, smelly hair and clothes and greatly increases the risk of lung cancer and other cancers, heart disease and circulation problems.

From being a 60 a day smoker, I managed to give it up. I can't pretend it was easy, but then again nothing in life is easy. The benefits were enormous. The method I employed was successful for me, I told myself that I wasn't giving up but I wouldn't have a smoke until 3.30 3 days later. When that time and day came, I said I wouldn't bother having a smoke just then but I'd smoke the day after tomorrow at 1.30 so on and so forth. This to me was pure psychology by not stopping but just putting it off. I was fortunate as well that into my second week of not having a cigarette I had booked a holiday on the Costa Del Sol. I was laid on a beach with the sea lapping at my feet I calculated that I could do this three times a year for a fortnight just for the cost of my cigarettes. I asked myself which I would prefer: smoking and killing myself or having a glorious holiday every 3 or 4 months.

It worked for me I would hope it would work for you.

Can't sleep?

When you can't sleep, everything seems like hard work. And as you get more tired, things can seem harder still. However, as frustrating as insomnia can be, there are some easy tips which can help provide you with good quality sleep.

Go to bed at a set time every night and get up at a set time every morning. Do this every day, even at weekends, and resist the urge to nap or sleep in. Regulating your body's sleep patterns is a good way to encourage healthy sleep.

Make your bedroom a place for sleep. Ensure all electric appliances, TVs, computers and CD players are kept somewhere else. Also make sure the room is dark and quiet to maximise your chances to relax and sleep soundly.

Try to avoid caffeine, nicotine and alcohol completely or at least from late afternoon, as these drugs are stimulants and will prevent you from sleeping.

Regular exercise will help you sleep as it raises endorphin levels, relaxes muscles and ensures health and well-being.

Make an effort to deal with any problems you might have during the day whilst you are wide awake and can do something about them instead of letting them creep into your thoughts at bed time.

If you are still being kept awake by worrying, make a list of your problems and possible solutions. Don't spend too much time over it, and the solutions don't have to be perfect – it should be enough to relax your mind into letting go, so you can fall asleep

If you know that you can't get to sleep, or back to sleep as the case may be, don't just lie there. Get up and do something, read for instance.

If problems persist, see your doctor, as there may be an underlying medical problem.

BABIES

Gone are the days when youngsters used to believe that children were born under gooseberry bushes or by just simply kissing a boy. But then again why are there so many unwanted pregnancies? Surely by now everybody knows that children are born as a result of sexual intercourse.

Babies are such wonderful things and shouldn't be born out of a mistake or born unwanted. No one should bring a child into this world at a disadvantage. But so many are.

We should all strive to give out kids a better start in life, more love and attention than we had and hopefully achieve more than we ever have. That should be our ultimate goal.

So why are so many born and end up in single parent families. Is it because of lack of knowledge, surely not in this day and age. Or is it because of selfishness and lack of thought. There are no excuses whatsoever to bring an unwanted child into this world. This is not to condemn every single parent family or to praise every dual parent family. Some single parents male or female do a tremendous job. And in some cases where a child has two parents its obvious that one of them would be better of not in the relationship. Some marriages are horrendous and play havoc with children's lives. Some marriages are made in hell, a lot of partnerships exist only in the interest of the children. But this is misguided, one loving parent is better than two bickering adults. The number of birth control methods is numerous. The obvious number 1 birth control is not to have sexual intercourse. No other method is as good or safe. All other methods have their faults and only abstinence (not having sex) is 100% sure.

Methods of Contraception

Contraception is any process used to prevent pregnancy. There are many different contraceptive methods available and different methods suit people at different times of their lives. The only 100 per cent effective contraception is abstinence and many contraceptives do not lower the risk of catching a sexually transmitted disease (STD).

Non-hormonal contraception works by either preventing sperm fertilizing an egg, or preventing the implantation of a fertilized egg into the lining of the womb. The main methods are:
1) Barrier methods
2) Intrauterine contraceptive devices (I.U.C.D.'s)
3) Natural family planning
3) Sterilisation

Physical barriers stop sperm coming into contact with the egg.

Male condom

A condom is a thin sheath, usually made out of latex, which is rolled on to an erect penis before sexual contact. They should not be used with an oil-based lubricant, such as Vaseline, because this can cause the latex to breakdown. Water-based lubricants such as K-Y Jelly, and spermicidal creams or pessaries are safe. Condoms can also protect both partners against certain sexually transmitted infections such as HIV, gonorrhea and genital warts.

Female condom

A female condom (Femidom) is a thin, soft, polyurethane pouch, which is fitted inside the vagina before sex. It has an inner ring that goes into the upper part of the vagina, and an outer one, which should be visible. The female condom is less likely to tear than the male condom. If used according to the instructions, the female condom is 95% effective.

The Diaphragm and the Cap

The diaphragm and cap are devices made of thin, soft rubber that are inserted into the upper part of the vagina to cover the cervix (neck of the womb). They act as a barrier to sperm. If used correctly, with spermicide, caps and diaphragms are 92-96%.

Sponge

This is a small sponge impregnated with a spermicidal gel or cream. It is moistened with water before use, and then inserted high into the vagina to cover the cervix. It needs to be left in place for at least six hours after sex, and can be left for up to 30 hours, although there is a risk of infection if left for longer than that. This method offers 70-90% protection.

Spermicides

These are creams, gels or pessaries (dissolvable tablets, inserted into the vagina) that contain a chemical that kills sperm. They can increase the effectiveness of barrier methods of contraception but they do not provide reliable contraception when used alone. Spermicides can be bought without a prescription at pharmacies. Some condoms have a coating of spermicidal lubricant.

The main advantage of a coil is that, once fitted, there is no need to worry about contraception. As long as the coil remains in place it can be left for three to ten years. They are up to 98% effective. If pregnancy does occur while using a coil, there is a small risk of an ectopic pregnancy. This is when the pregnancy develops outside the womb, usually in the fallopian tube. Although this is rare, it is dangerous, so if you miss a period, see your doctor.

The IUCD or coil

The intra-uterine contraceptive device (IUCD) or coil is a small plastic and copper device, which is fitted into the womb (uterus) by a doctor or nurse. It is designed to prevent the sperm meeting the egg, and may also make the egg move down the Fallopian tube more slowly and stop an egg setting in the womb.

An IUCD does not protect against sexually-transmitted infections.

There is a device available (called Persona) that measures body temperature and hormone levels in the urine. If used according to the instructions the manufacturer claims it is 94% effective. It may not work well in women who have short or long cycles, or in women using certain medicines such as tetracycline (an antibiotic) or women who have certain medical conditions. Check with a pharmacist.

The withdrawal method

This involves withdrawing the penis before ejaculation. It is not a reliable method and cannot be considered as contraception because some sperm can leak out of the penis before ejaculation.

Sterilisation

This is an operation to permanently prevent fertilization. It is therefore only recommended for people who are sure they do not want to have any more children. The failure rate of sterilization is around one in 2000 for men and about one in 200 for women. These operations are not easily reversible.

Men: Men are sterilized in a procedure called a vasectomy. This is a minor operation usually performed under local anaesthetic. It involves cutting or tying the tubes (vasdeferens) which carry sperm from the testicles to the penis.

Women: This is an operation performed under general anesthetic, usually as day case surgery. The Fallopian tubes are cut, tied or blocked, often through key-hole surgery. The alternative is a hysterectomy, removal of the womb after which pregnancy is impossible.

You can ask your GP, practice nurse or family planning clinic for more information on any method you are interested in.

Information is available from Family Planning Clinics: (08453101334).

The Pill

This tablet is taken once a day by women, and it contains two female-type hormones, an oestrogen and a progestogen. What these two hormones do is to stop a female from ovulating (producing an egg) each month. And if you don't ovulate, you won't get pregnant. In addition, the hormones thicken the secretions round your cervix thus making it more difficult for sperm to get through. Also, they make the lining of your womb thinner, so that it is less receptive to an egg.

Despite all the methods of contraception available, things can still go wrong.
Finding out you are pregnant when you have the support and wise-words of your family and a partner who is 100% supportive can be the most wonderful day of your life. On the other hand, if you are in a bed-sit, estranged from your family and the father of your child doesn't want to know, it can be the most traumatic and distressing day you are likely to have. If the latter is your circumstance then please believe all is not lost! The help available to you is enormous and it is you right to receive all the help that YOU are entitled to.

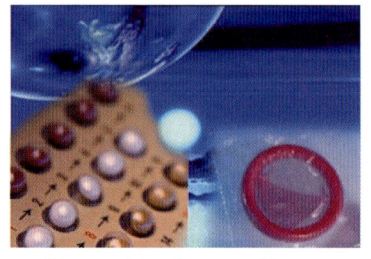

The earlier you explore all your options the better and easier it will be for you in the long term. Your decisions are yours and yours alone, you have several l options and a lot of thinking ahead and avenues to explore.

1) The first choice is the obvious one, to keep the baby.

The following organizations can help with ANY questions you may have:
To find your local pregnancy Counselling Centre visit:
Family Planning Association: *08453101334: alternatively* **www.fpa.org.uk**
Amica:*01316777800 alternatively:* **www.amicapcc.org**

2) If for whatever reason the first option is not a choice, another option would be to look at adoption. Again there are so many people out there who can offer you help and advice:

If you decide this option is the best for you, there is no hurry. Social Services will help you with the details and there is still time, even after the baby is born to change your mind. About 3-6 months after the birth if you have made it clear your choice is definitely adoption the n an adoption order will be agreed by the court and you no longer have any responsibilities, legal or other to the child.

Contact any of the organizations below for more information about adoption:

Adoption and Fostering: 02075932000 or: www.baaf.org.uk/
Adoption UK: 08707700480 or: www.adoptionuk.org.uk
(A full list of help organizations can be found here.)

3) Your final option would be termination. There are many reasons for considering each option and termination will occupy your mind just as much or even more as your other two options. Remember that shock can last for varying amounts of time, as will confusion. It is ok to be confused but when making your final decision you need to be deadly certain it is the right choice for you.

Call 08457304030 to make an appointment at a centre near you to discuss your options in detail.

British Pregnancy Advisory Service, Crisis Pregnancy and Abortion Help-lines: Tel: 01412265407   Help:08456038501   Care:08000282228
Alternatively call: Marie Stopes UK: 08453008090

All of the options are life changing but what is right for YOU is what is most important.

We should all strive to give our kids a better start in life, more love and at attention than we had and hopefully achieve more than we ever have. That should be our ultimate goal.

The obvious number 1 birth control is not to have sexual intercourse. No-other method is as good or safe. All other methods have their faults and only abstinence (not having sex) is 100% sure.

Gone are the days when youngsters used to believe that children were born under gooseberry bushes or by just simply kissing a boy. But then again why are there so many unwanted pregnancies? Surely by now everybody knows that children are born as a result of sexual intercourse? Babies are such wonderful things and shouldn't be born out of a mistake or born unwanted. No-one should bring a child into this world at a disadvantage. *But so many are!*

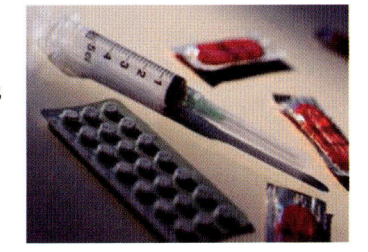

SEXUAL HEALTH

What are Sexually Transmitted Diseases (STDs)?

Sexually Transmitted Diseases (STDs) are diseases that can be transmitted through body contact during sex. They are caused by viruses, bacteria and parasites. They can also be known as Sexually Transmitted Infections (STIs) or by their old name Venereal Diseases (VD). There are at least 25 different sexually transmitted diseases. What they all have in common is that they can be spread by sexual contact, including vagina, anal and oral sex.

How do you know that you have an STD?

Anyone who is sexually active can be at risk from STDs. Some STDs can have symptoms, such as genital discharge, pain when urinating and genital swelling and inflammation. Many STDs, such as Chlamydia, can frequently be symptom less. This is why it is advisable to have a sexual health check-up, to screen for STDs, if you think you have been at risk. It can sometimes take a long time for STDs to display any symptoms, and you can pass on any infections during this time, further demonstrating the need to be tested and treated.

If you are in a relationship, and are diagnosed with an STD, it does not necessarily mean that your partner has been unfaithful. Symptoms of STDs can present themselves months after infection.

Are sexually transmitted infections treatable?

Yes. Most sexually transmitted infections are treatable.

Can you get sexually transmitted infections from oral sex?

Yes. Some sexually transmitted infections, including Chlamydia, Genital Herpes, Gonorrhoea, Genital Warts, Hepatitis B + C and HIV, are passed on through oral sex. To reduce the risk of infection, you can use a condom for oral sex. Dental dams (thin squares of latex) can also be used as a barrier during contact between the mouth and the vagina, or the mouth and the anus. Contact your local GUM (Genito-Urinary Medicine Clinic) for further details.

I've always used a condom, so does this mean I can't have a sexually transmitted infection?

Using condoms reduces the risk of sexually transmitted infections. However, different infections are spread in different ways, for instance condoms may not prevent the transmission of genital warts if other infected areas come into contact. We would suggest that you seek specialist advice from a health adviser at a GUM clinic.

Common Sexually Transmitted Diseases – The Basics

Chlamydia is the most common treatable bacterial STD. It can cause serious problems later in life if it is not treated. Chlamydia infects the cervix in women. The urethra, rectum and eyes can be infected in both sexes. Symptoms of infection may show up at anytime. Often this is between 1 to 3 weeks after exposure. However, symptoms may not emerge until a long way down the line.

Possible Symptoms

Women	Men
A slight increase in vaginal discharge – caused by the cervix becoming inflamed	A discharge from the penis which may be white/cloudy, watery and stain underwear
A need to pass urine more often/pain on passing urine	Pain and/or a burning sensation when passing urine
Lower abdominal pain	A painful swelling and irritation in the eyes (if they become infected)
Pain during sex	
Irregular menstrual bleeding	
A painful swelling and irritation in the eyes (if they become infected)	

Crabs or Pubic Lice are small, crab shaped parasites that live on hair and which draw blood. They live predominantly on pubic hair, but can also be found in hair in the armpits, on the body and even in facial hair such as eyebrows. They can live away from the body too, and therefore can be found in clothes, bedding and towels. You can have crabs and not know about it, but after 2 to 3 weeks, you would expect to experience some itching. Crabs are mainly passed on through body contact during sex, but they can also be passed on through sharing clothes, towels or bedding with someone who has them. There is no effective way to prevent yourself becoming infected, though you can prevent others becoming infected by washing clothes and bedding on a hot wash. Lotions can be bought from pharmacies and applied to the body to kill off the parasites. Shaving off pubic hair will not necessarily get rid of crabs

Genital herpes is caused by the herpes simplex virus. The virus can affect the mouth, the genital area, the skin around the anus and the fingers. Once the first outbreak of herpes is over, the virus hides away in the nerve fibres, where it remains totally undetected and causes no symptoms. Symptoms of the first infection usually appear one to 26 days after exposure and last two to three weeks. Both men and women may have one or more symptoms, including an itching or tingling sensation in the genital or anal area, small fluid-filled blisters that can burst and leave small sores which can be very painful, pain when passing urine, if it passes over any of the open sores and a flu-like illness, backache, headache, swollen glands or fever.

Genital warts are small fleshy growths which may appear anywhere on a man or woman's genital area. They are caused by a virus called the Human Papilloma Virus (HPV). Warts can grow on the genitals, or on different parts of the body, such as the hands. After you have been infected with the genital wart virus it usually takes between 1 and 3 months for warts to appear on your genitals. You or your partner may notice pinkish/white small lumps or larger cauliflower-shaped lumps on the genital area. Warts can appear around the vulva, the penis, the scrotum or the anus. They may occur singly or in groups. They may itch, but are usually painless. Often there are no other symptoms, and the warts may be difficult to see. If a woman has warts on her cervix, this may cause slight bleeding or, very rarely, an unusual coloured vaginal discharge.

Gonorrhoea is a bacterial infection. It is sexually transmitted and can infect the cervix, urethra, rectum, anus and throat. Symptoms of infection may show up at anytime between 1 and 14 days after exposure. It is possible to be infected with gonorrhoea and have no symptoms. Men are far more likely to notice symptoms than women.

Possible Symptoms

Women	Men
A change in vaginal discharge. This may increase, change to a yellow or greenish colour and develop a strong smell	A yellow or white discharge from the pens
A pain or burning sensation when passing urine	Irritation and/or discharge from the anus
Irritation and/or discharge from the anus	Inflammation of the testicles and prostate gland

Hepatitis causes the liver to become inflamed. There are various different types of hepatitis, the most common being hepatitis A, B and C. Each of these viruses acts differently. Hepatitis can be caused by alcohol and some drugs, but usually it is the result of a viral infection.

Thrush, also known as candiasis, is a yeast which lives on the skin and is normally kept in check by harmless bacteria. If this yeast multiplies however, it can cause itching, swelling, soreness and discharge in both men and women. Women may experience a thick white discharge and pain when passing urine. Men may experience the same discharge in the penis and difficulty pulling back the foreskin. Thrush can be passed on when having sex with someone who is infected, but also if you wear too tight nylon or lycra clothes or if you are taking certain antibiotics. Sometimes the cause may be unclear however. Transmission can be prevented by using condoms during sex and by men washing underneath their foreskin. Treatment for thrush involves taking or applying anti fungal treatments. Thrush can reoccur, especially in women.

How do they do the tests to find out if you've got a sexually transmitted infection?

There are different tests available. A full sexual health check includes an examination of genitals, a urine sample, taking a swab from the genital area and a blood sample. You may also be offered an HIV test but this will only be done if you agree.

Why is it important to know if you have an STD?

Many STDs are very infectious and can cause long-term or permanent damage, including infertility if left untreated. Many STDs can be easily passed onto sexual partners, and some STDs can be passed from a mother to her unborn child too. STDs can also aid the transmission of HIV.

HIV

What's the big deal about HIV/AIDS?

It's easy to think that AIDS is something for other people to worry about - gay people, drug users, people who sleep around. This is wrong - all teens, whoever they are, wherever they live need to take the threat of HIV seriously. To be able to protect yourself, you need to know the facts, and know how to avoid becoming infected.

Isn't it only a problem for adults?

No. HIV is a big problem for young people, as well as adults. In 2005, it is estimated that there were 2.3 million people under 15 living with HIV.

What's the difference between HIV and AIDS?

HIV is the virus that causes AIDS. AIDS is a serious condition in which the body's defences against some illnesses are broken down. This means that people with AIDS can get many different kinds of diseases which a healthy person's body would normally fight off quite easily.

How long does it take for HIV to cause AIDS?

The length of time between being infected with HIV and being diagnosed with AIDS depends on lots of different things. These days, there are many drugs that can be used to help people with HIV, and most doctors believe that a lot of people can be treated for a very long time. Many people do not know exactly when they were infected with HIV, and the length of time between this happening and them being diagnosed with AIDS can be very variable.

So how do you get infected?

HIV is passed on in the sexual fluids or blood of an infected person, so if infected blood or sexual fluid gets into your body, you can become infected. This usually happens by either having sexual intercourse with an infected person or by sharing needles used to inject drugs with an infected person. People can also become infected by being born to a mother who has HIV and a very small number of people become infected by having medical treatment using infected blood transfusions.
HIV can't be caught by kissing, hugging or shaking hands with an infected person, and it can't be transmitted by sneezes, door handles or dirty glasses.

What is 'safe sex'?

Safe sex means sexual activities which you can do even if one person is infected with HIV, and they definitely won't pass it on to the other person. Loads of activities are completely safe. You can kiss, cuddle, massage and rub each other's bodies. But if you have any cuts or sores on your skin, make sure they are covered with plasters (band-aids). Nothing you do on your own can cause you to get HIV - you can't infect yourself by masturbation.

What about using drugs?

The only way to be safe around drugs is not to take them. If you are on drugs you may take risks you normally wouldn't take, and you may have unsafe sex when you would normally be more careful. If you take drugs, you might find it more difficult to use a condom, or you might forget altogether. One of the most common drugs this can happen with is alcohol - if you're drunk, you might not always know what you're doing, or you might not care.
If you inject drugs, you should always use a clean needle, syringe and spoon, water, etc each time you inject, and never share any of these with anyone else. If you snort drugs, and you use a note or a straw to snort through, you shouldn't share it with anyone else, as blood can be passed from the inside of one person's nose to another.
If you have a tattoo or a piercing, you should make sure that the needles and equipment used are sterile. Ask the staff at the place you have it done about what precautions they use.

What is safer sex?

Safer sex also means using a condom during sexual intercourse. Using a condom is not absolutely safe as condoms can break, but condoms can be effective if they are used correctly.

Oral sex (one person kissing, licking or sucking the sexual areas of another person) does carry some risk of infection. If a person sucks the penis of an infected man, for example, infected fluid could get into the mouth. The virus could then get into the blood if you have bleeding gums or tiny sores somewhere in the mouth. The same is true if infected sexual fluids from a woman get into the mouth of her partner. But infection from oral sex alone seems to be very rare.

Can you get infected your first time?

Yes, if your partner has HIV and you have unsafe sex, then you can become infected.

Is there a cure?

There is no cure for HIV. HIV is a virus, and no cure has been found for any type of virus. Recently, doctors have been able to control the virus once a person is infected, which means that a person with HIV can stay healthy for longer, but they have not managed to get rid of the virus in the body completely.

How can I tell if someone's infected with HIV?

There is no way to tell just by looking at someone whether they are infected with HIV. Someone can be infected but have no symptoms and still look perfectly healthy. They might also feel perfectly healthy and not know themselves that they are infected.
The only way to know if a person is infected or not is if they have a blood test.

How can I get tested?

You may find it helpful to talk to an adult - perhaps a parent, school nurse or teacher may be able to advise you where you can have a test.. It's much better to talk to someone than to worry on your own. The clinic will suggest that you wait three months (or six in the US) after your last risky sexual contact before having a test. This is because the virus is difficult to detect immediately after infection.

What will they do?

Before they do anything, the doctor or nurse will ask if you're sure you want to have a test. They will usually take a sample of blood from you to examine.

If you also want to be tested for STD's, they may take a urine sample, or they might ask if they can take a swab from the vagina or penis. Some places can give you the results on the same day, in other places you may have to wait for a week or more. While you wait, you shouldn't have sexual contact with anyone.

I have HIV - what should I do?

If you have found that you have HIV, you will need to tell the people who you have had sex with and anyone you have shared needles with so that they can decide if they want to have a test. This can be a very difficult thing to tell someone. If you think you can't tell them, your doctor or nurse may be able to help you. Your doctor at the clinic should also be able to give you more advice about how to stay healthy. They will also be able to tell you if you need to have any other blood tests done, and talk to you about medication.

You cannot do a kindness too soon, for you will never know how soon it will be too late.

Sex

Sex is one of the most important functions that humans have. It's the most discussed subject and the least understood. It sells everything; it's bought and sold as a commodity. It provokes more arguments, and divides people more than any other subject barring religion, and has more taboos and myths than anything else. The list of myths and phobias is endless.

So what is considered normal sex?

It is a heterosexual couple having sex in the missionary position, 2.2 times per week?

OR

It's as varied as people's taste in food, clothes and music?

The answer is the latter.
It's an impossible question to answer, because people's tastes vary so much. Just to try and prove this, stand on any high street for fifteen minutes at it's busiest time and try and find two people identically dressed, but each and everyone think they are better dressed than any other.

Normal is what consenting adults do in the privacy of their own space, which does not hurt anyone.

You can't be forced into being homosexual, can you?

Homosexual sex, or sex with someone of the same gender, is not an illness or disease. You are born with sexual feelings that come to the surface, in most cases in a person's teenage years. Hormones dictate your feelings and desires. Never be ashamed of your sexuality, this just leads to all sorts of problems, including in the worst scenario, suicide. Some people, but few in number are bisexual. But you can't disguise your feelings.

Sex and Love

You know instantly if you are attracted to someone sexually, but don't confuse loving someone and being in love. There are all kinds of love, from loving a parent or sibling to loving an animal. Whilst loving someone isn't a prerequisite for sex, it is so much better if you do. One of the secrets of good sex is to be relaxed. Relaxation is the key, you can't "make love" if you are troubled or have a hang up in any way. You can get relieved, but it's not the same.

Masturbation

This means touching or stroking your own genitals for sexual pleasure/relief. This is perfectly harmless and many people do it just for the feeling it gives them. Other people don't masturbate at all or do not like it. Other names for masturbation are wanking or fingering, though there are many more slang terms.

Masturbation will not make you blind or infertile. People do it whether or not they're in a relationship – including women. It's just a natural way to get in touch with your body and the pleasure you can get from it.

You may want to do this with someone else present; this is known as mutual masturbation though this is usually done with someone you feel totally comfortable doing this with. Mutual masturbation is dangerous if you do not keep genitals apart, so keep body fluids separate and do not have unprotected sex afterwards.

Orgasms

There is no general rule of how many times a man can **ejaculate,** just as there is no rule as to how much we eat and what particular food we like. Some people have huge appetites and others peck away at food, each and every one of us is an individual, with likes and dislikes, fears and phobias. Trying to find an identical version of yourself is virtually impossible; you would find it easier to find a gold fish in the Arctic Ocean.

A lot of women never achieve **orgasm**. Whether this is to do with genetics or a selfish partner, you shouldn't beat yourself over the head. Many women just like the closeness and intimacy of sex and just want to be touched and caressed.

The **female clitoris** is that highly sensitive, and highly sought after, erectile sex organ. It's basically a fleshy bump, located at the top of the vaginal lips. Like the penis, the clitoris is packed with nerve endings and serves as the focus of stimulation of women, often resulting in orgasm. The best thing you can do is ask! If you're comfortable with your partner, and feel able to discuss such an intimate subject, then find out how she likes to be touched. With help, respect and experience, you'll soon find your way. Sex is at its best when both two people feel comfortable with the idea of getting intimate.

Possible reasons for not being able to orgasm

- ❖ Are you stressed out/exhausted? Simple fatigue can affect performance
- ❖ Have you been drinking heavily? Excess alcohol can delay or prevent climax.
- ❖ Is your partner making it obvious that they are dissatisfied? Such psychological pressure can also cause problems. Encourage you partner to be supportive, not critical.
- ❖ Are you taking any medication, or are you diabetic? Uncontrolled diabetes and the side effects of antidepressants or beta blockers may be to blame. See you GP.

Concerns

Mainly men are concerned with certain things,
for instance, the **length of their penis**, because they see confident men in the changing rooms proudly strutting around, whilst the majority are shielding their private parts behind their hands.
But man gets as much pleasure out of two inches, as someone with a larger than normal size penis. In fact a larger than normal penis can be a disadvantage, as some women could be hurt by the penetration.

Size doesn't matter for a purely personal point of view, just as large breasted women don't get more pleasure out of sex than small breasted women, and what is probably more important is foreplay. (**Foreplay** by the way is not 'Can I buy you a drink?')

Size is just cosmetic, so banish your fears about it. It's only important in your head. It's the same as having big muscles, or being a little bit frail looking. It's not a contest for size or staying power or how many times your best friend came. I know you feel so inadequate, finishing at your best twice and that's sometimes a bit of an effort.

If you listen and believe some of the stories, you would think of yourself as a complete failure. Just listen as you would to a fisherman describing the best catch he ever made, and always live by the rule **"A gentleman never tells"**.

Questions & Answers

But I'm a virgin!
Being a **virgin** isn't anything to be ashamed of. It doesn't make you any less of a man or woman, though a lot of lads lie about their sexual conquests in a bid to cover up their insecurities. Even if they are telling the truth, bragging about it doesn't show much respect for such an intimate act.

Can we have sex during her period?
Yes. Providing you're both comfortable with the idea, as there may be some menstrual bleeding, and you're sussed about safer sex. A woman isn't likely to get pregnant during her period, but there's always a chance – especially at the end of her menstrual cycle. What's more, unprotected sex increases the risk of exposure to sexually transmitted infections, period or not.

How can I tell if she's really had an orgasm?
Unless she's prepared to let you know, the truth is very difficult. Sure, you can look for little signs such as an increase in her breathing rate or a change in her body movement, but you'll never be sure if it's because she's having an orgasm or simply hoping that faking it will stop you looking so anxious! The only way to be sure is by talking about the issue with her. Find out what brings her to orgasm, and when, if at all. Ultimately, sexual communication is at the heart of any good orgasm, male or female – it's just a question of building up the trust and respect between you.

Surely size matters a little bit?
The size of a man's penis really doesn't have any bearing on his status as a lover. Women everywhere will vouch for the fact that a caring and considerate guy counts a lot more than a bloke with a big member and no brains. So chuck away your ruler, and start measuring up as a skilled, sensitive and rewarding sexual partner.

First Times...

Sex won't be perfect for the first time, but being open with your partner and talking to each other will make the whole experience better.

BOYS, you can practice putting a condom on (on your own) before you have full sex, so that you are ready and don't have to worry about pregnancy.

GIRLS equally only go for it if you are ready and make sure he wears a condom – as well as avoiding pregnancy it also reduces the risk of catching a sexually transmitted infection (STI).

BOYS may 'come' very quickly the first few times, but with practice you'll learn to control your ejaculation by thinking of non-sexy things. However, some find it very difficult to 'come' – usually because they don't feel relaxed, or because it isn't as pleasurable as masturbation.

GIRLS, you may bleed a little if your hymen was intact but it won't always hurt. Take it at your own pace, and make sure you are comfortable and relaxed, as it means less chance of any pain. Sex for girls can sometimes feel disappointing at first because it doesn't always stimulate the clitoris, but practice makes perfect.

If you are having sex regularly it might also be a good idea to seek out advise on various types of birth control.

Sex is legal at 16 in England, Scotland and Wales between a man and a woman, or between two men or two women. However, in Northern Ireland the legal age for both heterosexual and homosexual sex is 17.

BUT…Enjoy your childhood and don't be in too much of a rush to grow up!

The main rule to remember is that that if you think you might not be ready then you definitely aren't.

DO NOT be forced into anything.

It's worth remembering that the following are NOT good reasons to have sex:

- Because someone else wants you to
- Because someone says they'll leave you if you don't
- Because all of your friends are doing it so you think you should too
- Because you feel scared to say now

Rohypnol (Date Rape)

Rohypnol is a tranquilliser known as 'Roofies', 'R-2' and 'Date-rape drug'. It is a prescription drug though it is rarely prescribed. It is illegal to possess Rohypnol without a prescription. As with a lot of drugs it can be addictive. Side effects include headaches, muscle pain, confusion, hallucinations, convulsions and even seizures for up to a week after it has been taken.

If mixed with other drugs including alcohol it can be fatal.

It is commonly known as a 'Date-rape' drug as rapists use it to drug people before raping them. It is usually ingested without that person's permission by slipping it into a drink while the person isn't looking. However sometimes it is offered and sometimes even accepted by people who don't know the risks. Once a person has taken Rohypnol it is highly dangerous as it can not only cause all the health related risks of a tranquilliser but it can tranquillise a person against their will and cause partial or total memory loss a lot of the time that may never return and even altered behaviour. This is what makes it commonly used by rapists as they can slip it into a drink and rape someone without them being able to fight back or even remember what has happened. Even worse it can cause a person who would never normally go home with a person or who does not want to sleep with a person to say yes to sleeping with them when they really mean no! Rohypnol is extremely dangerous for all these reasons and more alarmingly rape under the influence of a 'Date-rape' drug such as Rohypnol is notoriously hard to prosecute as it can be hard to detect the drug seeing as the effects usually wear off in about 8 hours and due to the memory loss is not always remembered until it is too late.

Date-rape is virtually impossible to prosecute when a person has said yes to sex under the influence of Rohypnol when they really meant no as from the outside it looks as though that person has consented and this can be very distressing. Only 3 percent of all rapes are prosecuted mainly due to the fact that the majority of sexual violence does not involve strangers and so is far harder to talk about. Worryingly, more often than not people are raped by people they know and even trust. The stereotype of a stranger in an alley is far easier to report than if the attacker was a respected person in the community, a friend or even a relative.

The best bet to avoid anything like this happening to you is to keep an eye on what you are drinking at all times. NEVER leave a drink unattended and NEVER accept drugs even if it is from someone you know.

Rapists are people who force other people to have sex with them against their will or have sex with people who are under 16 years of age (the age at which a person is allowed to consent/say yes to having sex). If a person under 16 says yes to having sex with someone over 16 that doesn't make it legal as the person under 16 does not by law have the right to say yes. When this happens it is called 'statutory rape' and is a crime for the person over 16 as they have the responsibility by law. The person under 16 is not considered guilty of a crime as by law they have not been given the responsibility to make the decision to have sex by law. The law protects persons under 16 from having to make the choice to have sex responsibly as there are so many unhealthy reasons that influence the decision such as peer pressure, attention, feeling more grown up, hormones influencing a decision that may later be regretted.

Giving someone drugs without their knowledge or permission is always a serious crime but it is then made even more serious if you do this with the intention to take advantage of them. If someone says no to sex with you giving them drugs to change their mind is pathetic, against the law and punishable with 14 years in prison.

All incidences of rape or attempted rape should be immediately reported to the police or someone in authority. You're not only helping yourself but will be increasing awareness and helping prevent someone else from suffering the same fate.

PROBLEMS AT WORK

After playground bullying in childhood and unrequited love in your teens, your life's woes continue in the work place.

From time to time you will get problems at work. The first thing you will have to do is to address them and tackle them head on. If it's your fault be honest with yourself.

Admit that you need help. Bad news rarely comes out of the blue, when you feel that things are going wrong, pre-empt them by owning up to your shortcomings and asking for support and guidance to overcome them. The worst thing is to sit dreading the day when the manager calls you into his or her room for that fateful word.

If you are in danger of losing your job or disciplinary action is being considered you are entitled to representation.

Legal Representation "As a worker the law says that you have a legal right to be accompanied in disciplinary hearings by a trade union official or a fellow worker of your choice", Trades Union Congress's Worksmart website www.worksmart.org.uk Ask to see a disciplinary procedure when you're asked to attend a hearing.

Performance complaints about your general performance are trickier to handle. Don't be too defensive. "The obligation is not simply on the employee to improve, it's also on the employer to indicate why you aren't doing what's required and how they can help you to achieve you targets."

Don't get in a huff with your manager Whether you get demoted, put on report or get a severe ticking off, the weeks afterwards are crucial to your career and require a great deal of character.

Make sure it doesn't become a personal issue. Management usually want a settled and happy team and don't want change for changes sake.

Relationship Break-up

Often when a relationship finishes, women suffer months of heart-ache, whilst men move on swiftly over a pint with their mates.

The Scientific Explanation?

According to studies at the Medical University of South Carolina, women actually experience a change in their brain patterns after an emotional break-up that causes this behaviour, with brain scans showing a drop in motivation, emotion and attention span. Gradually, though, these brain patterns return to normal, and as they do, girls are able to bounce back and move on. So heartache does heal with time!

However, if this process is taking too long to handle, there are some ways to give your brain a helping hand.

Be good to yourself

When relationships fall apart, it's easy to think it was someone's fault, or that you aren't handling the situation as well as you should be. However, it is important to give yourself time to deal with what has happened, as pretending everything's fine or giving yourself a hard time will only stop you recovering properly.

Call on friends

For the first few weeks after a break-up, it is OK to call friends late at night, miserable and crying. Allow them to look after you, either by calling round with a bottle of wine and chocolate, having you to stay or listening attentively at the end of a phone. Not only will this help you deal with the initial pain, but also it will probably make you and your mates closer, which is just what you need!

Let go of memories — Be it giving him a box filled with his t-shirts you used to sleep in and other knick knacks he left around, or by chucking out photos, letters and trinkets that you gathered throughout the relationship, it is important to do away with relationship souvenirs as they will only prolong your pain.

It might be worth keeping one photo of your ex-beloved, however, so that in many years to come, you can look back to the good old days and remember the guy you were once mad about.

Get your cash sorted — Whilst it's boring, not to mention the last thing you'll feel like doing, it is vital you separate your finances, for instance a joint mortgage, a shared bank account or a holiday fund, or your money situation could get very messy.

Seek out the help of a financial advisor to do it properly, let your ex know what's happening and break the financial ties.

Revenge — Should the relationship have ended badly for you, try to hold back on any vengeful thoughts, as they will only make you seem desperate and crazy. Instead, concentrate on getting back on your feet as a singleton, enjoying life to the full and being happy – the best revenge!

Be selfish — All relationships involve compromise, where each of you stops doing things at the request of the other. However, now that you're single you have no-one to answer to, so whether you wanted a hamster (but he was allergic) or you wanted to see Rome (but he had already been) or you are a keen rock music fan (which gave him a headache), now is the time to get on and do all those things you love and he hated. Be selfish!

Don't stay friends

Whilst exes can be friends, it only works when those painful feelings have long since gone. So, whilst the thought of ending it forever seems hard, thinking you can stay in each other's lives by being friends won't work. And if it does, it'll only last until:

- One of you finds a new partner
- One of you thinks it would be OK for friends to sleep together
- One of you thinks being friends is one step back to being back in a relationship
- One of you thinks you should stop being friends – And the whole painful process starts all over again.

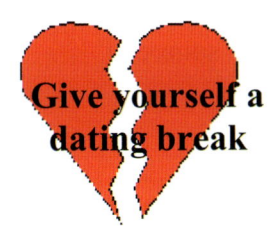

Give yourself a dating break

Whilst it may be tempting to start dating, there is no point doing so unless you're ready. Chances are you'll treat your new man very badly, whether you're constantly comparing him to your ex or if you're with him just to show your ex what he's missing out on. The truth is if you aren't ready for a new relationship you are leading the guy on, so wait until you're ready and give you're potential suitors a chance!

Contentment is the only real wealth.

Coping With Death

If somebody you know or even somebody you don't know dies it can be very hard to deal with. You may have a mix of feelings all at once or you may not feel anything. It is not unusual to feel confused, angry, hurt or even guilty.

It can help to talk to someone about your loss. You could talk to a friend, relative, religious or community member or someone from an organisation that is there to help, (see below). It may be hard to talk to someone or the person you may speak to may be a little awkward when you do. Don't be put of if they do act like this - it is usually just because they do not know what to say.

Allow yourself as long as you like to grieve; this can be days, weeks, months or even years. Grieving is the process of accepting that a person is dead and coming to terms with it. This process varies from person to person, but keep hold of your good memories as they can become a source of comfort to you.

Cruse Helpline
0870 167 1677
(Charged at national rate)

Cruse Youth Bereavement Line
(aimed at people between 12 and 18 years old)
Freephone 0808 808 1677
Mon-Fri 9.30-5pm

Samaritans
08457 909090

Depression

Everyone can feel low once in a while, but it is important to recognise the difference between that and depression. Common symptoms of depression are:

- Exhaustion on waking
- Disrupted sleep, sometimes through upsetting dreams
- Early morning waking and difficulty getting back to sleep
- Doing less of what they used to enjoy
- Difficulty concentrating during the day
- Improved energy as the day goes on
- Anxious worrying and intrusive upsetting thoughts
- Becoming emotional or upset for no particular reason
- Shortness of temper, or irritability
- Change in appetite

You may not experience all of these symptoms, and you might experience different ones altogether. However, with so many patients with depression being wrongly diagnosed, it is important not only to see a doctor, but also to be completely honest with them about how you are feeling.

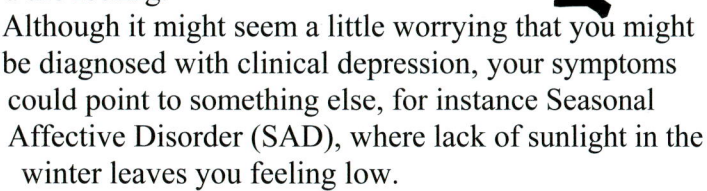

Although it might seem a little worrying that you might be diagnosed with clinical depression, your symptoms could point to something else, for instance Seasonal Affective Disorder (SAD), where lack of sunlight in the winter leaves you feeling low.

And if you are diagnosed with a form of depression, you also shouldn't see it as a life sentence. There are many treatments available for depression, from special light boxes for SAD sufferers to alternative treatments, such as aromatherapy. There are also various anti-depressants available and, if you are uncomfortable taking such medication, you could always try a herbal remedy, such as St John's Wort.

However, make sure you consult your doctor to ensure you find the right treatment for you.

Finally, if you just need someone to talk to and don't want to confide in friends or family, there are various organisations you could call, for example the Samaritans (08457 90 90 90).

You could also attend a local help group.

Bullying

HELP STAMP OUT BULLYING IN THE SCHOOLS AS WELL AS IN THE WORKPLACE

There are lots of different types of bullying. It could be being called names or ignored like you don't exist or being physically hurt in some way. People sometimes put up with bullying but they shouldn't. It is not acceptable and is punishable by the rules and regulations of all respectable organisations not to mention the law if it occurs outside of an organisation such as a school, college, university or place of work. People who bully often do it to make themselves feel powerful or better about themselves by putting someone else down. Bullies sometimes bully out of jealousy of the person they are bullying or to appear powerful to others. Though it can be difficult to talk about bullying you must remember it is not your fault. Bullies are pathetic if they choose to spend their time hurting others whether emotionally or physically it is a serious matter that should never be tolerated. You can get support if you are being bullied from friends, family, carers, teachers, supervisors, union members (if it is someone in the workplace who is bullying you including your boss or someone above you) or helplines like the ones listed below:

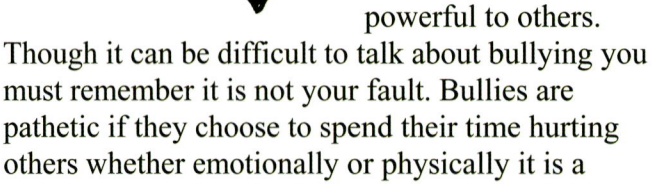

Anti Bullying Campaign

Tel: 020 7378 1446

Kidscape

Tel: 020 7730 3300

Hygiene

If on leaving home your first residence is in a shared house or flat, hygiene is probably the most important aspect of your relationship with your fellow residents.

And the biggest problem could arise in the kitchen, this could become disaster zone.

It may become contentious and you could become a social outcast but all members of the community should put cleanliness as the number one priority. Once a kitchen starts to get dirty it rapidly goes downhill and food poisoning and stays in hospitals are inevitable. If standards are set high initially people tend to keep up standards. But straying away from this is very, very easy.

It is essential therefore that people not only take responsibility for their own cleaning duties but other peoples too.

Worktops cutlery cooking utensils should be cleaned thoroughly after use and inspected on every occasion before use. It's far, far, better to clean twice and be sure, rather than finish up with food poisoning.
It would be a good idea to have some kind of rota system but everyone should be made aware of the basic principals of hygiene.

Food obviously should be kept in the fridge whenever possible. Fry ups and the reheating of food is to be avoided as much as possible. Extra care needs to be paid to sell by dates on food. Do not use any food past this date and check food nearing the end of its shelf life before use.

Clean hands are at the forefront of any battle against infection especially after using toilets. As you can imagine toilets are the number one source of infection special attention should be given to toilet seats and the handle. Everyone should get into the habit of washing hands after using these facilities.

REMEMBER TO STAY CALM AND CONTACT THE EMERGENCY SERVICES
FIRST AID

Bleeding

Major Bleeding

Immediately seal the wound with the casualty's own hand or your hand (preferably gloved, but ideally with a clean pad or bandage). If an object is protruding then apply pressure around the sides. Never attempt to remove the object. Elevate the wound so gravity can assist. If the bleeding is arterial it will be bright red and spurt out. If this is the case, raise the bleeding point above the level of the heart. If this fails apply extra pressure.

Lay the casualty down in order to reduce shock and risk from fainting. Dress the wound with a bandage firmly. Should bleeding seep through, apply a second bandage.

A tourniquet is dangerous and should not be used in first aid. It should only be used by medical professionals.

Internal Bleeding

Lay the patient down and encourage them to keep still. Treat for shock, and send to the hospital or for a doctor.

> Stomach: Blood is usually vomited if there is internal bleeding in the stomach. It will look dark brown in colour.
Do not feed or put anything into the patient's mouth.

> Nose: Sit patient up and loosen all tight clothing. Apply cold water compresses to nose and back of the neck and encourage the patient to breathe through the mouth.

Shock

Keep patient warm and comfortable. Lie flat on back with foot of bed or stretcher raised to keep head low. Loosen tight clothing and give warm sweet tea, cocoa or coffee except when there is an internal injury suspected. Send for doctor or ambulance.

Broken Bones

Steady and support the injured limb, preventing movement. Place the casualty in the most comfortable position.
Do not move the casualty unless they are in danger.

Burns

Cool the affected part with cold water until the pain is relieved. This should normally take around 10 minutes. (20 minutes if a chemical burn).

If possible, remove rings or any jewelry quickly before the affected part, e.g. finger, swells.

Cover the affected area with a CLEAN cloth, or, if properly cooled, a polythene bag or cling film is ideal.

Do not remove clothing as this has been sterilised by heat. Burned areas not covered by clothing should, if possible, be covered with sterile gauze dressing. Treat for shock.

Choking

Help by getting the head low for gravity to take effect. Encourage casualty to cough. Administer up to 5 slaps on the back, directly between the shoulder blades, each one sufficient to dislodge the obstruction, checking the casualty's mouth after each slap.

OR

Administer up to 5 abdominal thrusts (not to be used on infants or pregnant women). Standing behind the person, place a fist onto the upper abdomen. Grasp your fist with your other hand. Pull sharply in and upwards towards the diagram, forcing air out of the lungs.

Electric Shock

If the casualty has been electrocuted and is still attached to the current, you should try to break their contact with it. Insulate yourself from electric shock by standing on a phone directory before helping them. Then move the electric cable away from the casualty, using a rolled up newspaper or a dry piece of wood, such as a broom handle.

Fainting

Press head well down between knees. If this is not successful, lay the patient down, undo tight clothing and ensure airways are clear.

Fractures and Sprains

Do not move until limb is firmly strapped. If it is a leg, fasten to the sound leg. If it is an arm, fasten to the body.

Heart attack

Symptoms of a heart attack are usually a crushing pain in the chest. This can be mistake for indigestion. The pain often wraps around the body like a tight band. It may also spread to the arms, throat, neck, jaw, back or stomach. The person may also be breathless. Their complexion will be very pale and the casualty will show signs of sweating and appear weak and dizzy.

What should I do?
Obviously your first reaction should be to call for emergency medical assistance, especially if the pain has lasted for more than 15 minutes.

When ringing for the ambulance, try to stay calm as they will require as much information as possible. Do not be concerned if the questions appear to be taking a long time…by now the ambulance will already have been dispatched.

Sit the casualty up in a comfortable position, propped up with their knees bent and supported underneath. Try to constantly reassure them.

Check for a heart beat

Look, listen and feel for normal breathing, coughing or movement. Watch out for poor skin colour, blueness of the lips and cold skin. If there are no obvious signs, or you are unsure…

Start chest compressions

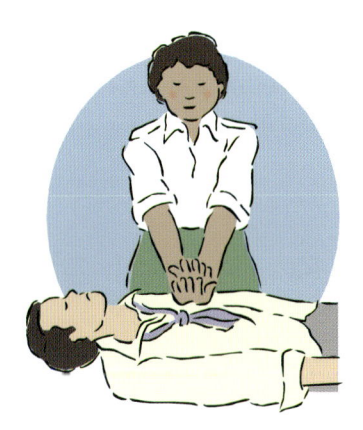

Find the lower half of the breast-bone. Place the heel of one hand there and the heel of the other hand on top. Interlock your fingers. Now depress and then release the breast-bone four or five centimetres. Fifteen times. Do this at the rate of 100 per minute. That's faster than one per second.

REPEAT 2 BREATHS AND 15 COMPRESSIONS CONTINUALLY. Don't stop until the casualty shows signs of life, or professional help arrives or you feel exhausted.

Once signs of breathing are detected, the casualty should always be turned to the recovery position, providing other injuries permit.

For children (under 7 years old) and babies, adjust the strength by which you blow or push on the chest: gentle blow and one hand for children, puff of air and two fingers for babies.
Complete at a rhythm of 1 breath to 5 compressions.

Insect Bites and Stings

Remove sting if possible. Application of carbonate of soda will give relief. A touch of TCP or Germoline will also help.

Poison

The first two things you must remember, if in a situation involving poison, are firstly, to seek medical attention as soon as possible, and secondly, DON'T PANIC!!! Often fear can produce similar symptoms to actual poisoning, making an accurate diagnosis difficult.

Poison that has been swallowed

If it is an acid, give an alkali, e.g. chalk or magnesium. If it is an alkali, give an acid, e.g. vinegar or lime juice. If you haven't go these in your first aid cabinet, give copious amounts of cold water or milk to drink.

Poison in the eye

Remove contact lenses if worn. Gently flush the eye for approximately 10 minutes with *slightly* warm water. Using a clean glass pour a stream of water down on to the eye from about 3 inches above the eyebrow. Do not use eye drops unless advised to by a professional medic.

Poison on the skin

Remove contaminated clothing and rinse affected skin with large amounts of water. Once don, rinse the same area again, but this time with hand soap and *warm* water.

Inhaled poison

Get to the fresh air as soon as possible. Open windows, doorways etc to permit ventilation and extract poisonous fumes.

Non-corrosives

If there is no burning of lips or mouth, give an emetic, such as a tablespoon of mustard, or two tablespoons of salt in a half pint of lukewarm water. It is essential that you save the poison container for examination by medical professionals so take it with you if you go to hospital.

Medicines and Travelling

If you are planning a trip abroad:

- Pack your medicines carefully. Keep them in their original, correctly labelled container and carry them in you hand luggage. Always carry spares, especially if your illness is life threatening.
- Some prescribed medicines may contain controlled drugs, which may need a license to be taken out of the country. If you are in any doubt whatsoever contact the Home Office Drug's Branch on 02072178457.
- It would be advisable to obtain a letter from your doctor, detailing what your medication is and your clinical diagnosis.

Some things to consider:

Some types of travel vaccines need to be given well in advance of your holiday, your doctor or local pharmacist will advise you as to which vaccines you will need for your trip and what arrangements you need to commence treatment in good time.

Your local pharmacist will also advise you about appropriate anti-malarial medication, which you may be able to purchase from the pharmacy or get on a private prescription from your doctor. All anti-malarial medications need to be started before your departure, some as early as two or three weeks before you leave.

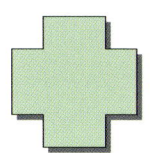

The type of travel vaccine and jabs that you need to depend on the countries you intend to visit and the length of your stay. It is essential to take advice from your doctor.

In hot climates drink plenty of fluids, particularly after exercise. Isotonic drinks that replace the salt lost through sweating are ideal, but water is also sufficient. Avoid alcohol on flights and in the sun, no matter how tempting - even if it's complimentary.
Don't spoil a holiday for the sake of a freebee!

HOLIDAY FIRST AID

Athletes Foot

These sore itchy spaces between the toes are worse in summer because the fungus that causes them thrives on sweaty skin cells. Wash your feet daily and dry with tissues and put anti-fungal foot powder between the toes. Go barefoot as much as possible and wear leather or canvas shoes, preferably sandals.

Heat Exhaustion

In its mildest form can give you headaches, dizziness or a shivery, sick feeling caused by losing too much salt and water from the body through excessive sweating. Drink plenty of water or fruit juice with half a teaspoon of salt added per litre. Severe salt and fluid loss can cause heat stroke with a rapidly rising fever and faintness. Call a doctor or emergency services at once because this can be a medical emergency. Try to cool the person with cold wet towels and a fan.

Intertrigo

This is a raw, red, weepy rash in the crease under the breasts or around the crotch. It is caused by the chafing of warm skin, and can become infected by bacteria or yeast. It is more likely in overweight people, or women whose breasts are large or slack. An anti-fungal cream from the pharmacist will help clear it.

Prickly Heat

This outbreak of frenzied itching and tiny blisters usually happens in sweaty places, such as the inner forearms, armpits, the hollows above the collar bone and under the breasts. It is caused by sweat pores which become internally water-logged. The remedy? To use an after shower astringent, wear loose fitting clothes and sit in the shade.

Stings and Bites

The smell of lemon wards off the mosquito. Mix one tablespoon of lemon juice with on egg cup of olive oil and rub on. Bee stings and ant bites should be dabbed with one tablespoonful of bicarbonate of soda (TCP or Dettol) mixed in one cup of ice cold water.

Sunburn

To prepare your skin take 100g of vitamin B6 and para/aminobezoic acid a week before going on holiday. It is also essential to use suntan creams. If you do burn, mix two parts cider vinegar to one part olive oil to keep skin moist.

Upset Stomach

Hot sun and an unfamiliar diet, as well as dodgy water, can make your stomach susceptible to bugs. By eating raw garlic and live yoghurt containing good bacteria, you can help to create an antiseptic in your stomach lining. If you are struck down, relieve pain with an hourly drink of boiled water with half a tablespoon of powdered cinnamon. To ease diarrhoea, mix two tablespoons or cider vinegar in one glass of water to drink before each meal. Hot and cold compresses applied to the stomach soothe nausea. A cool water compress will reduce a high fever. Finally, drink plenty of bottled water with one tablespoon of salt and two tablespoons of sugar to each glass. High street chemists sell excellent remedies for upset stomachs which you can buy before you leave.

Danger! Medicines!

Whilst it may seem reasonable to trust your doctor, don't be afraid to question the medication he prescribes. If you don't do this, you could be one of the 1.7 million Britons being taken into hospital for problems caused by medicines.

Things you should know

The name of the medicine you need to take.

What it does
You should enquire what the medicine does and how it will make you better. If you won't get worse without treatment, and may get better on your own, the doctor may decide you don't need to take anything.

If it causes any side effects.
It's possible that the risks of the medicine outweigh the possible benefits.

How long you should take it for?
For antibiotics, it is usual to be advised to finish the course, whilst other medicines, such as painkillers, you should stop taking once you feel better.

How and when
Make sure you understand when you should take it (before meals/in between meals/before bed), the correct dosage and how often you should take the medicine.

Exceeded dose
Always find out what you should do if you accidentally overdose.

Interactions
Make sure you tell your doctor about any other medications you are taking, DO NOT expect him to know. This includes herbal remedies, contraceptives etc. Also discover whether you are able to drink alcohol with your medicine and if there are any other foods/drinks you should avoid.

Colds and Influenza

<u>The Facts</u>
- Viruses cause Colds and 'Flu'
- Antibiotics do not kill viruses
- Don't expect your doctor to prescribe an antibiotic – it won't work!
- Remember viral colds are self limiting and will get better without treatment
- However you may feel unwell for 7 days or more

So remember NOT EVERY BUG NEEDS A DRUG!

<u>What should you do?</u>
- Stay warm and rest
- Drink plenty of fluids
- Take paracetamol to help control aches, pains and fever

For any other symptoms you can consult your local pharmacy
If, after a week, your illness does not seem to be getting better or you think you are developing additional symptoms, which give you concern, you can ask your local pharmacy for more advice.

Antibiotics – The Facts

<u>Fact!</u> Antibiotics stop working if we over use them
Bacteria can become resistant to antibiotics if they are over-used and they can stop working over time

<u>Fiction!</u> There's no harm in taking antibiotics just in case… Antibiotics kill the 'good' bacteria inside you, and taking them can give you diarrhoea, nausea and a nasty case of thrush! So if you don't need them, don't take them!

<u>Fiction!</u> The doctor will always give you antibiotics if you ask for them
The doctor will always give you antibiotics if he/she thinks you have an infection they can help, but not if you're suffering from a virus. Antibiotics don't work against a virus.

<u>Fact!</u> The pharmacist could help you if you have a virus The pharmacist will tell you about products to ease your symptoms. Just ask!

BREAST EXAMINATION

This is an important thing to do if you are a woman, or even if you are a man though it is rare in men under 60. Breast examinations are carried out to check for lumps and bumps that could be unhealthy including ones that might contain cancer cells that are the cause of a very dangerous disease. It is important to know what your breasts are like normally and to check regularly for bumps. 90% of all breast cancers are discovered at home and the earlier the better.

Breast Cancer

Breast Cancer is the most commonly diagnosed cancer in women – nearly 1 in 3 of all cancers in women occurs in the breast. The risk of getting breast cancer in your lifetime if you are a girl is 1 in 9. The risk to someone under 25 is far less than the risk to someone who has been through the menopause, though 2,200 of the 8000 people diagnosed each year are in there 20's and 30's. It is not usually passed on from parents to children as only 5-10% of cancers are found in people with a family history of cancer. Breast cancer can be fatal if left for too long. The sooner it is discovered the better. Breast cancer can be treated, depending what stage the cancer is in you can either operate and take out the tumour (usually if it is at an early stage), undertake chemotherapy or operate to take off the whole breast (known as a mastectomy). Operating on a small tumour that does not require removing the whole breast is usually for small tumours have not 'metastasized'. This means have not become active and spread to other parts of the body, which is a very big problem and can be fatal. If cancer has begun to metastasize or in some cases it is ok to undergo chemotherapy instead. This is a lengthy process of medication that can make you feel very sick as it is attacking cells in the body itself in order to kill the bad cancer cells.

Chemotherapy can cause the hair to fall out so it is advisable to look for a wig if you wish to have one afterwards just in case and so you can get used to wearing it. A myth surrounding breast cancer is that you cannot breast feed if you have it as it can pass on to your child. There is no proof of this and scientists believe cancer cells are not passed on in breast milk.

Home Cooking.

One of the greatest deterrents to leaving home is to go without any cooking skills whatsoever, the thought of not coming home to one of Mummy's hot and tasty meals is terrifying, but have no fear, help is at hand.

Celebrity chefs my ....

Who are the best cooks? Your Mum or Dad, they're the ones you will miss the most not these overpaid over-hyped TV posers.

Put six of our Mothers against Anthony, Ainsley, Gary or Gordon making a steak and kidney pie and see whose makes your mouth water the most.
Here are a few tasty meals, very easy to make with inexpensive ingredients and make you feel as if you've never left home.

Meats

Beef, Pork and Lamb

The following chapters are not to make out the case for meat eating at the expense of vegetarians or animal rights, but just to try and explain the various cuts and dishes that can be made from animal products.
We will not delve into exotic gourmet dishes or foreign cuisine as with everything in life moderation is paramount.
For instance, too much red meat can be bad for you, but can also be a very good source of protein and sustenance.
The most popular red meat is of course Beef from the cow.
Various cuts are used for very different dishes, we will also feature in this article, Pork and Lamb products, cuts and uses.

Getting the Balance Right

Balance your meat meals with plenty of starchy foods such as rice, pasta, noodles, bread (preferably whole grain varieties) or potatoes.
Also have generous helpings of salad and vegetables for every meal and include fruit throughout the day for snacks and deserts.
In the butchers shop or supermarket look for meats labelled lean or extra lean and meat products labelled low fat.
Avoid adding fat during cooking by grilling or dry-frying rather than frying in added oil or fat.
Variations will occur in cooking and serving.
Red meat is a very good source of iron.

Most recipes are equally delicious with equivalent cuts of either beef lamb or pork. The choice is yours.

BEEF:

Mystified in the meat aisle? Here's how to choose the right cut for the job.

Brisket: Cuts of beef from the chest region; these cuts are used to make corned beef or smoked for barbecue

Chuck: Cuts of beef from the shoulder region or front end; usually used in cooking roasts and commonly referred to as pot roasts.

Flank: Cuts of beef usually found as steaks; this is the cut most often used

Loin: Cuts of beef from the back region; cuts are very tender; most of the steak cuts like strips, t-bones and porterhouses come from this region.

Round: Cuts of beef from the back end region; usually used in cooking roasts and commonly referred to as rump roasts.

Sirloin: Cuts of beef from the small back region; sirloin cuts are very versatile and can be found as steaks and roasts.

General Beef Buying Tips:

Price: Since the most tender cuts make up only a small proportion of a beef carcass, they are in greatest demand and usually command a higher price than other cuts

Roasts and steaks should be firm, nor soft or squishy feeling

Be certain that the packages don't contain any excess moisture. This moisture could mean that the product has been above 38-40 degrees F for a period of time, and will usually not taste as good as meat that has been well chilled.
Be sure that the package has not been damaged and that the meat is cold and wrapped securely.

<u>Always check the 'sell-by' date on the label and only purchase on or before that date</u>.

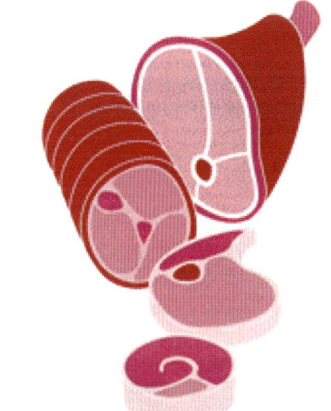

Beef and pork cooking tips

- Here's how to bring out the succulent juicy best in you beef and pork.
- Leave a thin layer of fat on steaks, chops and roasts during cooking to seal in juices.
- Trim fat after cooking (fat means flavour).
- For better browning, pat dry beef steaks, pork chops, cubes and roasts with a paper towel.
- Salt beef or pork, after cooking or browning. Salt draws out moisture and inhibits browning.
- Turn all steaks, roasts and chops with tongs, do not use a fork! This pierces the meat and allows flavour full juices to escape.

No need to wonder anymore if your meat is still good and fit to eat. For the best possible flavour and freshness here is how long you can store your favourite cuts of beef in the refrigerator or freezer

	Refrigerator (2 degrees centigrade)	**Freezer** (-10 degrees centigrade)
Steak	One to two days	Nine to twelve months
Hamburgers	One to two days	Six to nine months
Roasts	One to two days	Three to four months
Once Fully Cooked keep for		
Steak	Three to four days	Three to four months
Hamburger	Three to four days	Three to four months
Roast	Three to four days	Three to four months

If you would like to know the nutritional content of the different meats the simple table below will help you.

Beef Steaks

Type of Steak	Griddling	Frying/ Griddling/ Dry Frying	Stir Frying	Roasting	Casserole Stew/ Pot Roast/ Braising
Sandwich 1-2mm	1-2mins each side	45 secs-1 minute each side	Not Recommended	Not Recommended	Not Recommended
Thin cut sirloin steaks 1.5cm	2-4 mins each side	2-4 mins each side	Cut into strips 2-4 mins + 2 mins with veg	Not Recommended	Not Recommended
Sirloin Rump Ribeye 2cm	Rare:2 ½ mins Medium:4 mins Well Done:6 mins Each side	Rare:2 ½ mins Medium: 4 mins Well Done:6 mins Each side	Cut into strips 2-4 mins + 2 mins with veg	Not Recommended	Not Recommended
Fillet, T-Bone, frying, medallions 2-3cm	Rare:3-4 mins Med:4-5 mins Well Done:6-7 mins Each Side	Rare:3-4 mins Med:4-5 mins Well Done:6-7 mins Each Side	Not Recommended	Not Recommended	Not Recommended
Stewing steak (chuck blade)	Not Recommended	Not Recommended	Not Recommended	Not Recommended	Oven Temp: Gas Mark 3, 170°C, Stew for 2-3 hours
Braising steak (shin, leg, neck)	Not Recommended	Not Recommended	Not Recommended	Not Recommended	Braise 1 ½ - 2 hours

Pork Cuts

Type of Pork Cut	Grilling	Frying/ Griddling/ Dry Frying	Stir Frying	Roasting	Casserole Stew/ Pot Roast/ Braising
Escalopes 0.5cm	2-4 mins each side	1-2 mins each side	Not Recommended	Not Recommended	Not Recommended
Fillet sliced (tenderloin) 1-1.5cm	3-5 mins each side	2-4 mins each side	Cut into strips 2-4 mins + 2 mins with veg	Not Recommended	Not Recommended
Loin, leg, shoulder, valentine, medallions 1-2cm	6-8 mins	6-8 mins	Cut into strips 2-4 mins + 2mins with veg	Oven temp: Gas mark 4-5, 180°c, 350°F 25-30 mins turn halfway through	Leg, shoulder, steaks Oven temp: Gas Mark 3, 170°C, 325°F Braise/Casserole 1-1 ½ hours
Loin, leg, shoulder, valentine, medallions 2cm+	8-10 mins Each Side	8-10 mins Each Side	Cut into strips 2-4 mins + 2 mins with veg	Oven Temp: Gas Mark 4-5, 180°C, 325°F 25-30 mins turn halfway through	Leg, shoulder steaks: Oven temp: Gas Mark 3, 170°C, 325°F Braise/Casserole 1-1 ½ hours

Pork Chops- Loin, chump, spare-rib 1-2cm	6-8 mins Each side	6-8 mins Each side	Not Recommended	Oven Temp: Gas Mark 4-5, 180°C,325°F 25-30 mins turn halfway through	Oven temp: Gas Mark 3, 170°C,325°F Braise/Casserole 1-1 ½ hours
Pork Chops- Loin, chump, spare-rib 2-3cm	8-10 mins Each side	8-10 mins Each side	Not Recommended	Oven Temp: Gas Mark 4-5, 180°C,325°F 25-30 mins turn halfway through	Oven temp: Gas Mark 3, 170°C,325°F Braise/Casserole 1-1 ½ hours

	Lamb cuts				
Type of lamb cut	Grilling	Frying/ griddling/ deep frying	Stir frying	Roasting	Casserole/ Stew /pot roast/ braising
Steaks Leg (bone-in and boneless) Chump, shoulder, loin. 2cm thick	4-6 mins each side	4-6 mins each side	Not Recommended	Not recommended	Not recommended
Steaks as above over 2cm thick	6-8 mins each side	6-8 mins each side	Not Recommended	Not Recommended	Not Recommended

Loin, chump, cutlets 2cm	Not Recomm-ended	6-8 mins each side	Not recomm-ended	25-30 mins	Not Recomm-ended
Leg, neck fillet 1 cm	Not Recomm-ended	Not recommended	2-4 mins with veg	Not recomm-ended	Not recomm-ended
Joints; leg, shoulder, breast shanks, rack.	Not Recomm-ended	Not Recomm-ended	Not Recomm-ended	Medium: 25mins per 450g (1lb) +25 mins - 70-75°C Well-done: 30mins per 450g (1lb)+30 mins - 75-80°C	25-30 per 450g (1 lb) + 25-30 mins
Burgers 1-2 cm	Not Recomm-ended	4-6 mins each side	Not Recomm-ended	15-20 mins each side	Not Recomm-ended
Mince	Not Recomm-ended	4-6 mins each side	Not Recomm-ended	Not Recomm-ended	Not Recomm-ended

Sugar is a type of bodily fuel, yes, but your body runs about as well as a car would on it.

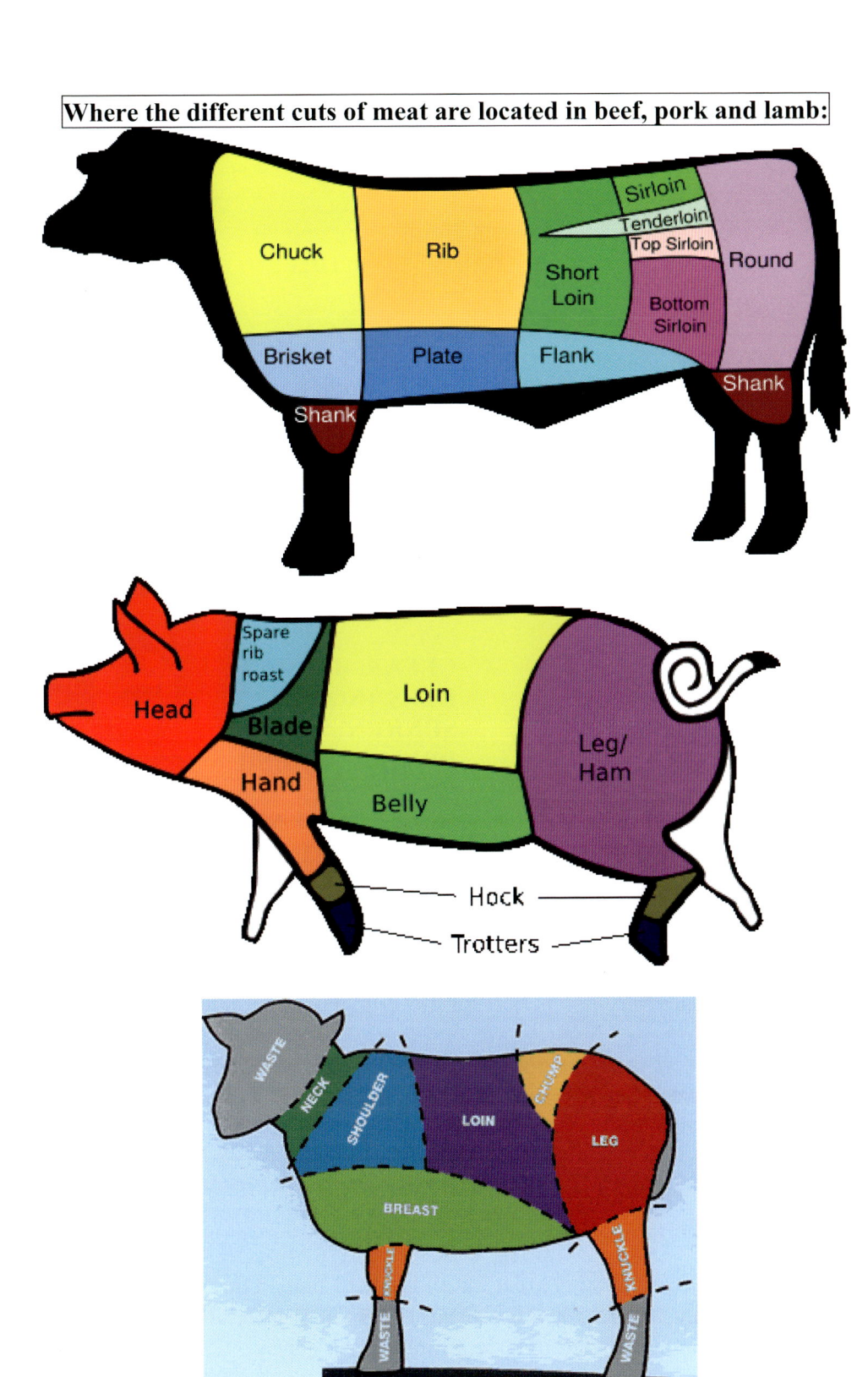

Where the different cuts of meat are located in beef, pork and lamb:

FISH

Fish is such a nutritious food and a non-fattening one. It would probably be more popular if the public at large knew how to cook it.

Believe me, there is no mystery; the small effort in trying will be worth it. The following are the most popular and the easiest to cook; we will get to the fancier fish later. Of course fish is best when it is fresh, things to look for are:

CLEAR, BRIGHT EYES, (NOT SUNKEN).
BRIGHT, REDISH GILLS.
SCALES NOT MISSING. MOIST SKIN, (FRESH FISH SHOULD ALWAYS FEEL SLIPPERY).

COOKING FISH:

BROILING: Thick fatty fish is best for broiling. Try salmon, tuna or halibut.

GRILLING: This is the most popular way of cooking fish. Fish steaks are great grilled. White fish needs basting first and some fish needs to be turned half way.

SHALLOW FRYING: Heat oil first and lightly dust with flour. Turn fish halfway through.

POACHING: This method is great for all types of fish. You need approx 70ml – 1/8th pint water. Try a few drops of lemon or milk. Even white wine or cider can add different taste. Simmer fish gently.

BAKING: Pre-heat oven and place fish in a dish. Sprinkle with lemon juice for flavouring, cover and place in centre of oven.

STEAMING: Place fish in between two plates or in a steamer over pan of boiling water, bring to the boil.

MICROWAVING: Place fish in a dish, add 2 x 15ml spoon of liquid, cover and cook then stand for 2 minutes.

DEEP FRYING: Heat oil, coat fish in batter or breadcrumbs and fry until golden brown.

TIP! Fish is cooked when it looses its slightly translucent appearance and turns white/opaque in colour.
You would be surprised that micro waving fish is a great way to cook, simply add less water than you would in other methods.

Fish has good fats and many health benefits. It is easy to prepare and general cooking time is ten minutes for every inch of thickness.

SHOPPING FOR FISH

Fish can be available fresh, frozen or canned.
Your Fish Monger or Supermarket should stock a wide selection of each of the groups of fish. Ask for assistance whilst selecting, your supplier will be happy to prepare fresh fish for you in the way that you want it.
Note that one species of the same type can be substituted for another.
For example when following a recipe for Cod, which is a large, round fish, you may substitute it with another large, round fish such as Coley or Pollack.

COOKING TIPS

Fish can be cooked quickly and in a variety of ways. Here is an easy guide to help you when cooking fish.

GRILL — Pre heat grill to a medium setting. Some fish will be turned during cooking. Baste white fish during grilling.

SHALLOWFRY — Dust the fish with seasoned flour. Heat the oil and fry the fish, simmer gently for the recommended time

POACH — Using 70ml water and a few drops of lemon juice, add the fish and simmer gently for the recommended time

BAKE — Pre heat oven to 190 degrees c (375f), Gas mark 5. Place the fish in a suitable dish and sprinkle with lemon juice. Cover and place in oven.

STEAM — Place the fish between two plates or in a steamer over a large pan of boiling water.

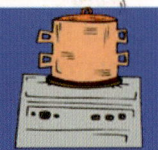

MICROWAVE — Time based on 800 watt microwave. Place the fish in a suitable container, add 2 tablespoons of water. Cover and cook

DEEP FRY — Heat the oil to 180 degrees-190degrees c\350-370 f. Coat the fish in batter or breadcrumbs and fry until golden brown.

STORAGE

To ensure that your fish always tastes great you should observe the following storage instructions.

Remove fresh fish from its original wrappings. Rinse in cold water, pat dry, cover and place towards the bottom of the fridge.
Always store cooked, ready to eat fish such as smoked mackerel, prawns and crab, at the top of the fridge, separated from raw fish. Store fresh and smoked fish separately to avoid mixing flavours.

Fresh fish, unless it states on the packaging, is best eaten within two days.

Frozen fish should be stored at -18 degrees C or colder.

Defrost fish overnight in the fridge; otherwise cook the fish from frozen, adding approximately 2 minutes to the cooking time.

It is recommended that if fish is stored at -18 degrss C, the maximum storage period should be no more than three months for smoked fish, shellfish or oil-rich fish and 4 months for white fish.
If in doubt always consult your fish supplier.

Quick Reference:

Shellfish are extremely versatile and there is a large selection available. They are split into two main groups. Crustaceans are those with legs such as crabs or lobster. And there are Molluscs that have no legs such as scallops, mussels or oysters.

White fish are divided into two types; round and flat. Large, round white fish such as Cod and Coley are usually sold as steaks, fillets or cutlets. The small round species such as haddock are usually sold as fillets. With flat fish, the larger species, such as Halibut and Turbot are sold whole, in fillets and as steaks. Smaller flat fish such as Lemon sole are usually sold whole, trimmed or filleted.

Oil-Rich fish such as Herring and Mackerel are rich in OMEGA 3 fatty acids, which have been shown to have a lowering effect on blood fats. This is effective against cholesterol and heart attacks. Oil-Rich fish are also a great source of vitamins A and D.

HALIBUT
Bake, Braise, Grill, Poach, Shallow Fry,
Stir Fry, Steam, Microwave.

PLAICE
Bake, Braise, Grill, Poach, Shallow Fry, Stir Fry, Steam, Microwave.

HAKE
Bake, Braise, Grill, Poach, Shallow Fry,
Stir Fry, Steam, Microwave.

HADDOCK
Bake, Braise, Grill, Poach, Shallow Fry, Stir Fry, Steam, Microwave. Available as cold smoked, as smoked haddock fillets, golden cutlets and Finnan haddock.

COD
Bake, Braise, Grill, Poach, Shallow Fry, Stir Fry Steam, Microwave.

LEMON SOLE
Bake, Deep Fry, Grill, Poach, Shallow Fry, Stir Fry, Microwave.

COOKING TIMES

All timings are given in minutes and are to be used as a guideline as thickness of fish and cooking appliances vary.

170g/6oz PORTIONS	GRILL	SHALLOW FRY	POACH	BAKE	STEAM	MICRO-WAVE	DEEP FRY
STEAKS							
COD	10	8	6	20	15	2	–
HAKE	13	8	7	20	15	2	–
HALIBUT	8-10	6-8	8	20	12	1½-2	–
SHARK	8-10	6	–	22	–	1½-2	–
SWORDFISH	8-10	6-8	–	22	–	2	–
TUNA	8	6-8	–	20	–	2	–
FILLETS							
COD	8	9	8	20	15	2	4-6
COLEY	10	10	8	20	15	2½	4-6
HUSS	8	8	7	25	18	1½-2	6-8
HADDOCK	10	10	8	20	15	2	4-6
ORANGE ROUGHY	8	8	8	25	18	2	–
SNAPPER	10	6-8	8-10	20	18	3	–
WHOLE OIL-RICH FISH (CLEANED)							
HERRING (340g/12oz)	6-8	7-8	8-10	20-25	–	2	–
MACKEREL (340g/12oz)	8-10	10-12	–	20-25	–	3	–
SARDINES	6	8	–	–	–	–	–
SPRATS	–	4	–	10-15*	–	–	–
OIL-RICH FILLETS							
HERRING	4-5	–	–	–	–	1½-2	–
MACKEREL	5	7-8	–	15-20	–	1½-2	–
KIPPERS	5	–	3	10	–	1½	–
WHOLE FLAT WHITE FISH (CLEANED)							
LEMON SOLE (340g/12oz)	10	8-10	–	20-25	–	3	–
PLAICE (340g/12oz)	8-10	6-8	–	20	–	3	–
FLAT WHITE FILLETS							
LEMON SOLE	5	4-5	5	15-20	10	2	4-6
PLAICE	5	4-5	4	15	9	2	4-6
HALIBUT	10	8	10	25	15	3	–
SMOKED FISH FILLETS							
COD	8	8-10	6	20	15	2½-3	–
HADDOCK	8	8-10	6	20	15	2½-3	–
OTHER FISH							
MONKFISH TAIL (340g/12oz)	7-9	–	–	30	–	2-3	–
SKATE WINGS	7-8	7	6	20	15	2	–

EGGS

Eggs come in four sizes. Very large 73g and over, Large 63-73g, Medium 53-63, Small 53g and under.

The four types of eggs are:
FREE RANGE,
 (Which relate to or are produced by chickens that are allowed to move around freely and are not kept in cages.
ORGANIC, FRESH EGGS and OMEGA 3 EGGS, (which helps maintain a healthy heart). As part of a healthy diet, we should be eating more Omega-3 fatty acids such as those found in Omega 3 enriched eggs. One Omega 3 egg provides you with at least two thirds of your recommended daily intake and helps maintain a healthy heart and circulatory system and also is a major constituent of the brain and nervous tissue. Omega 3 is also found in oily fish, seeds and some cereals. Omega 3 eggs look, taste and are as versatile as other eggs. They can be boiled, scrambled, poached, fried and used in baking and are suitable for everyone, just look for Omega 3 on the packaging.
Eggs are packed with a wide range of nutrients including protein, essential vitamins A, D & E and B group as well as minerals iron, phosphorus and zinc. They are relatively low in saturated fat, making them healthy fast foods for all the family. Eggs are also low in calories with only 78 calories per medium egg…so they are great if you are on a diet.
Other interesting facts for eggs are that shelled boiled eggs will keep for 5 days in the fridge.
Also, the freshness of an egg is dependant on many things. Don't always rely on supermarket dates etc, the most efficient way to tell if it is still fresh is to crack it open and see!

The more an egg holds its' shape in the pan the fresher it is.

One widely believed myth is that brown eggs are better for you than white eggs. The colour of an egg is dependant on the hen that lays it. Hens with white feathers and earlobes lay white eggs and hens with red feathers and earlobes lay brown eggs.

Eggs come in two qualities…A and B grade.

TIP: How to stop eggs cracking when putting into hot water.

Even the best eggs sometimes crack when put into hot water to stop this happening as much prick the rounded end of the shell with a pin. This lets air escape from the cold egg when it is added to the hot water. Also adding a teaspoon of salt to the water helps stop egg leaking out of the shell.

Carefully remove the eggs from the pan after cooking then tap at the pointed end to stop it cooking too much inside.

SUPERBLY SCRAMBLED EGGS

Scrambled eggs are one of the quickest and most convenient ways of cooking eggs.

2 Large Lion Quality Eggs
Pinch of salt and pepper
2 teaspoons of Milk (optional)
Knob of butter or low fat spread
Slice of buttered toast to serve (optional)

METHOD
Gently beat the eggs together with salt and pepper. Add 2 t-spoons of milk to the eggs for a softer result.
Melt a knob of butter\low fat spread in a non stick pan over a medium heat. When sizzling, add the egg mixture and stir with a wooden spoon.
Continue to stir the eggs for 1-2 minutes, scraping the egg off the base of the pan as it sets.

When the most of the egg has set, remove the pan from the heat and continue to stir for 30 seconds until fully scrambled. Serve immediately with a round of buttered toast.

PERFECTLY POACHED EGGS

1 Large Lion Quality Egg
Water for boiling
Pinch of salt
Dash of vinegar
Warmed buttered muffin or toast (optional)

Fill a large pan with 5cm (2") of water. Add a pinch of salt and a dash of vinegar to help set the egg. Bring the water to a gentle boil. Crack the egg onto a plate and then tip it into the water. Set a kitchen timer for one of the timings below:

3 minutes for a completely runny egg, 4 minutes for a slightly set yolk with runny middle, 5 minutes for a firm egg yolk

When cooking time is complete, carefully remove the poached egg from the boiling water using a slotted spoon and place on kitchen paper to drain. Serve immediately with warmed buttered muffin or a slice of buttered toast.

BOILED EGG

Boiling an egg is simple once you have mastered the basics!

Ingredients:
2 Large Lion Quality Egg
Water for boiling
Pinch of salt
Buttered toast cut into soldiers (optional)

METHOD

Place an egg into a small pan. Cover with at least 2.5cm (1") of water, add a pinch of salt and place the pan on a high heat.

When the water is almost boiling, gently stir the egg and set a kitchen timer for one of the timings below:

3 minutes for a really soft boiled yolk and set white
4 minutes for a slightly set yolk and set white
5 minutes for a firmer yolk & white
6 minutes for a hard boiled with lightly soft yolk
7 minutes for firmly hard boiled

Reduce heat slightly to keep water bubbling but not fast boiling and stir the egg once more.

THE ORIGINAL OMELETTE

Ingredients:
2 Large Lion Quality Egg
Pinch of salt and pepper
1 T-spoon full of cold water
25g (1 oz) butter

METHOD
Gently beat the eggs together with salt, pepper and a tea spoon of cold water.

Melt the butter in a medium frying pan over a high heat.

When the fat is bubbling, pour the egg mixture into the centre of the pan and cook over a high heat for 1-2 minutes.

As the egg begins to set, use a spatula to push the set egg towards the omelette centre.

Continue this action until the egg mixture is set.

Cook the set omelette for another minute, then loosen the edges with a spatula and fold the omelette in half.

Great food is like great sex, the more you have, the more you want.

Which potatoes?

Potatoes may appear the same in a shop but when making a portion of chips, using the wrong kind could leave you with a pan of mush!

Potatoes, along with eggs, are probably the most versatile of our staple foods and choosing the right one is essential.
If you fancy chips for tea then the types listed above are the best to use…
Potatoes should be peeled and cut into the preferred thickness, then soaked in clean water for approximately half and hour. This will get rid of any excess starch. Then they need to be dried and placed into boiling hot fat or oil…180 degrees is the ideal temperature.
Your chips will be ready when they start to rise to the top of the pan. Place them on kitchen paper to drain the oil/fat. Then serve them and enjoy them!

Home made chips, you can't beat them!

Boiled or mashed potatoes need the same cooking times and preparation as chips. Peel and cube the potato then place them in a pan of boiling water. When done, a fork with a little pressure should easily pierce the potato. For mashing drain potatoes into a bowl and just add a little warm milk and a knob of butter while you mash with a masher or as a substitute, a large fork.

Jacket potatoes can be served with basically anything and there are many ways to cook them.

However my particular favourite is as follows:
Scrub a large potato and pierce all over with a fork, microwave on full for between 2-3 minutes. Brush with oil then place on tin foil.
Put in oven on gas on 220 or gas mark 7 for approximately 1 hour (depending on the size of pot). Wait until the outside of the spud is crisp and brown and is soft all through.
Gently cut the potato and fill with a tasty filling.
These could be: Philadelphia cheese, Baked Beans, Grated Cheese or Sour cream and butter.

Be as imaginative as you like!

New potatoes are actually immature potatoes harvested in the early spring and early summer. They have flimsy, thin skins which you can remove with your fingers. They have a high moisture content, low starch and often, (but *not* always) a waxy texture. Examples of waxy new potatoes are:
Jersey Royal, Record, Rocket and most salad potatoes.
My favourite and the ones recommended by the Potato Marketing Board are:

FOR BOILING OR MASHING

SAXON   NADINE

FOR ROASTING

WILJA   ROMANO

FOR BAKING

CARA

MARFONA

FOR CHIPPING

MARIS PIPER

KING EDWARD

Maris Piper and King Edward are a very versatile potato and can be used for most of the purposes above.

FOR SALADS

NICOLA

CHARLOTTE

Poultry

Cooking poultry is relatively easy simply anyone can roast a great chicken but there is a lot more to it than that. This page is one pf the most serious in this book.

Poultry can be prepared in many different ways. It is virtually a staple diet in most kitchens because of this you need to learn everything you can that the methods you use of handling and cooking poultry you are doing the best you can to protect the health of housemates.

Below is the essence of what you need to know if you're going to be a good cook and not threaten the well being of your friends and family.

Poultry can be purchased in many forms, fresh or frozen whole or cut up bone in or boneless, chicken particularly had become increasingly popular because it is considered in expensive and healthier than red meat and on top of that tastes very good. To meet demand chickens are raised indoors in huge chicken houses that may contain as many as 20, 000 birds they are fed are a mixture composed primarily of corn and soy bean meal. Animal proteins, vitamins, minerals and small amounts of antibiotics are added to produce quick growing healthy birds.

Chickens raised this way unfortunately do not have the flavour of chickens that area allowed to move freely – free range chickens – that is why people are increasingly drawn to buying free range chickens. They are allowed unlimited access to the area outside the chicken house they are fed a vegetarian diet (no animal fat or by-products) without antibiotics. This is obviously a more humane growing method although they are more expensive it is well worth it as a taste is so much better.

Hazards

Poultry is potentially a hazardous food it is highly perishable and particularly susceptible to contamination by salmonella bacteria.

Before cooking poultry it is critical that it is stored at the correct temperature fresh chickens can be stored on ice at around 32-34 degrees farenheight for up to 2 days. Larger birds can be stored for up to 4 days at the same temperature. Frozen poultry should be kept at below 0degrees farenheight (the colder the better) and can be frozen for up to 6 months. Chickens should be thawed gradually preferably under refrigeration, allowing 2 days for large chickens but less for joints and pieces.

Never, never attempt cooking chicken that is still partially frozen.
It is impossible to cook the product evenly and the areas that were still frozen may not reach temperatures necessary to destroy harmful bacteria.

Partially cooking poultry one day and finishing it later is completely out of the question, bacteria will thrive under such conditions

DO NOT DO IT

Always wash your hands, chopping boards, knives and anything else that comes in contact with the poultry, with soap and warm water immediately to prevent contamination.

Vegetarians

Vegetarians can be separated into four main types:

Type 1) Semi vegetarian -These 'vegetarians' eat all types of foods – including meat. However, these individuals limit the amount of animal products they consume.

Type 2) Lacto vegetarian - Individuals in this group are a step up from the semi vegetarians. They avoid all animal products except dairy in their diet.

Type 3) Lacto-ovo vegetarian - This type of vegetarian diet excludes all meat, but includes dairy and eggs. (Not too different from Type 2)

Type 4) Vegan -   These are the 'hard core' vegetarians who avoid all animal products in their diets, such as meat, dairy and eggs. The vegan diet relies on lentils, beans and soy products etc.

Whilst it may seem unlikely, vegans and vegetarians are able to maintain a well rounded diet without any animal products by relying on the protein and essential nutrients provided by vegetables, beans, nuts and soy products.

Aim to eat very colourful vegetables such as broccoli, cucumbers, carrots etc. These types of veggies are especially high in vitamins, calcium, beta-carotene, zinc and many more essentials.

Beans and soy products (tofu, soy milk) are excellent sources of protein. And don't think that these types of protein are inferior to animal protein – they're not. And even better, in comparison to animal protein, they are much lower in saturated fat – the type of fat that's bad for you!

Below are some very basic food examples and their protein content. It's also worth remembering that the recommended daily allowance of protein for men is only 63 grams, and for women just 50 grams.

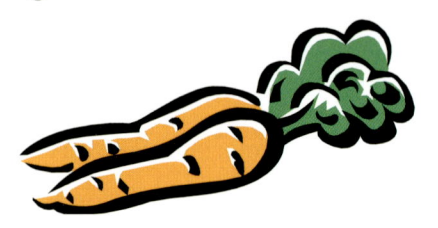

Animal Product	Protein/ grams	Vegetarian alternative	Protein/ grams
3 oz baked chicken	28	Soya beans	29
3 oz roast pork	28	Chick peas	15
3 oz steak	24	4 oz Tofu	15
Fish	21	Spinach	11
Minced beef	20	Broccoli	10
1 Glass milk	8	T.V.P	8.5
Medium egg	6	Beans baked	5

Beauty is what the heart tells the brain.

WINES

Wines are probably only second to sex in their myths and mysteries. But there is no mystery to wine, just drink what you like and what you can afford. Don't be put off by the many names, origins and years; good wines don't necessarily need to be expensive or old.

Just be confident when it comes to ordering wine…after all the people at the table next to you probably know less than you do!

Understanding wine is sometimes a real quandary, and if you're dining out with a partner possibly for the first time it can be a totally devastating experience and could at the very least be an embarrassment or the end of a relationship.

Don't be put down by the wine snob or be made to feel inadequate, remember it's you that's paying the bill.

Relax, don't be pressurised into making a quick decision. It's imperative that you give the right impression that you know a little about wine. With just a few pointers you will learn to control the situation. The right wine can make good food taste even better. By taking a sip of wine it will cut through the oils on your palette making each mouthful even better.

Sniffing corks, swirling around the mouth and spitting out we will leave to the wine snobs and experts. The old chestnut that wine is a living thing and needs to breathe is the most ruinous and much believed by the decanter brigade. There are those who open bottles on the morning of a smart dinner believing mistakenly that their three pound ninety nine bargain will mutate given exposure to the air into something magnificent. It wont, it will most certainly oxidise just as the cut apple turns brown, and taste flat.

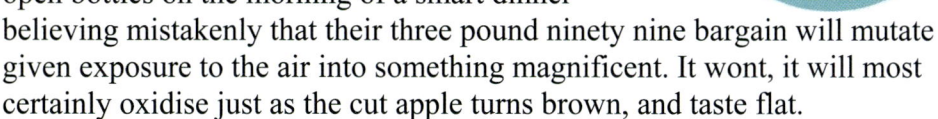

Other common fallacies include the notion that vintage and single variety wines are made exclusively from the grapes declared on the label. In fact lots of wine producing countries allow as much as fifteen percent from other years and varieties. I hate the idea too that the more expensive a wine is the better it must be or that white wines and champagne need hours of chilling in the fridge, when really its only thirty minutes that is usually required.

My other pet hate is that all reds are best served at room temperature, when lighter reds like a Baujolais often taste better when slightly chilled. Or that red wine never goes with fish.

We will just concentrate on three basic types of wine: **red, white and sparkling.**

Red wine should be served a few degrees below the room temperature of a centrally heated room, so keep them cool until ready, most reds under 5 pounds can be served cool so give them 40-50 minutes in the fridge or about five minutes in iced water, while white wine is best served chilled. Of course in a restaurant the temperature of your wine will be in the hands of the waiter so no worries there. Party wines whatever their colour should be served cooler than usual, because they will soon warm up. Iced water is the most effective way of chilling bottles. Some shops sell ice and chiller bins (or use the bath/sink). Don't over-chill expensive fine whites because you will numb their aromas and flavours. If using a fridge, allow two hours for whites, remembering that fridge temperatures vary. Outdoors is a good place to chill wines in winter. Sparkling-wine bottles are made of thick glass, so they take longer to chill.

Bordeauxs, South African Pinotage, Chile and Australian Cabernets should be served chilled.

While Champagne should be served on a bed of ice

Buy for Value

Unless you're on a tight budget don't just settle for the house wine. In most restaurants, the house wine has the highest margin and as a result they generally offer poor value. If you dig in to your pockets a little and spend a few more pennies there's a much better chance you'll get the right wine. Don't be scared to ask the wine waiter (or sommelier as they are known in posh restaurants) for their advice. If the chef's on hand, then they can also be useful sounding board to offer you advice on what will go best with your food. Don't forget that a restaurant's staff will know the menu a lot better than you (well at least they should do) and they can often help you to find the best match. Cheers!

Generally grilled steak goes well with a more astringent, more tannic red wine. The bitterness imparted from the grill can be offset with this combination. Acidic white wine goes well with shellfish, whereas spicy dishes are best accompanied by a spicy wine like for instance a Muscat or Gewürztraminer. Sweet wine with sweet food.

Long Shadow Chardonnay – is a refreshing summertime, or anytime, Australian white wine the colour of pale straw and has nectarine and peach aromas. This wine goes well with seafood, chicken and salad

Jacob's Creek Riesling – is a crisp, elegant Australian white wine with a fresh, floral bouquet with aromas of lime blossom and citrus. Now, doesn't that just trip of the tongue! Great with salmon, chicken, spicy food – almost anything, in fact.

Jacob's Creek Shiraz Cabernet – Can you smell the plum and blackberry in this velvety crimson red wine? Maybe with a touch of vanilla oak? You'll certainly taste it. Great with red meat and cheese.

Anapi River Pinot Noir – The vineyards of this New Zealand wine are next to a river and therefore don't need irrigating. This medium bodies wine has a wonderful jammy aroma of cherries and cloves. Summer and Christmas rolled into one, goes great with chicken.

It is recommended when dining in an ethnic restaurant, i.e. French or Greek, to drink French wine or Greek wine because generally over centuries they will have learnt which wines go best with their authentic food.
Three types of good red wine that are universally accepted and go with most foods are; **Australian Shiraz, Cabernet Sauvignon and Rhone.**

Remember:
The most important factor is the temperature of the wine. For wine to be refreshing, it has to be served chilled, even red. And it also must have good acidity which is that mouth-watering quality that cuts through the rich flavours and makes the wine seem gluggable and moreish. A special favourite of many are the aromatic, uncomplicated whites, such as Savignon blanc and fruity, not too tanic reds, such as pinot noir, that can take a chill without loosing their point. Plus, of course, those chewy reds that are customary with flame-charred meals.

Sausages

The great British banger is probably the best culinary invention in the world and is envied by every chef who wishes he had invented this delicious treat. Sausages come in all kinds of sizes, flavours and textures. Some contain abnormal amounts of fat others too many breadcrumbs and some just plain awful! But find a good sausage and this is a real dish to set before a king. It is well worth spending time seeking out a sausage maker, your local butcher is a good place to start.

The usual method for cooking sausages is to fry them or grill them.
For those amongst you who are health conscious, grilling is the best option. Always remember to prick your sausage before grilling.

To fry heat some oil in a pan and fry the sausage for 15 to 20 minutes or until golden brown. Keep turning regularly to make sure they cook evenly. To grill just turn once, 10 minutes each side on a medium heat.

It is essential that they are served with mashed potatoes or into a fresh bread roll with lashings of brown sauce.

Conversions

OVEN TEMPERATURES

°C	Fan Oven	F	Gas
130	110	250	½
140	120	275	1
150	130	300	2
160	140	325	3
180	160	350	4
190	170	375	5
200	180	400	6
220	200	425	7
230	210	450	8
240	220	475	9

METRIC/ IMPERIAL WEIGHT

15g	½ oz	250g	9oz
25g	1oz	275g	10oz
50g	2oz	300g	11oz
75g	3oz	350g	12oz
100g	3 ½ oz	375g	13oz
125g	4oz	400g	14oz
150g	5oz	425g	15oz
275g	6oz	450g	1lb
200g	7oz	1kg	2lb 4oz
225g	8oz	1.8kg	4lb

METRIC/ IMPERIAL LIQUID

25ml	1fl oz	350ml	12fl oz
50ml	2fl oz	375ml	13fl oz
75ml	3fl oz	400ml	14fl oz
125ml	4fl oz	425ml	15fl oz
150ml	5fl oz	450ml	16fl oz
175ml	6fl oz	475ml	17fl oz
200ml	7fl oz	500ml	18fl oz
225ml	8fl oz	550ml	19fl oz
250ml	9fl oz	600ml	1 pint
300ml	10fl oz	1 litre	35fl oz
325ml	11fl oz	1.5 litre	2 ¾ pints

Shepherds Pie

Serves 2
250 grams minced beef
1 small onion peeled and chopped
1 clove of garlic (optional)
Chopped tomatoes
½ tablespoon of mixed herbs
1 tablespoon olive oil
3 medium potatoes, peeled diced
Salt and pepper to taste

Heat the oil in a large pan, add the onion and garlic and cook for 3 minutes. Add the meat and cook for a further 9-10 minutes. Then add all the other ingredients except for the potatoes. Simmer for 10-15 minutes.
Meanwhile, cook then mash then with a little butter and milk. (A fork passing easily through the potato means they are cooked)
Pour the meat into an oven proof dish and spread the potato over the top to cover the meat. Put under a hot grill or in a hot oven until brown on top

Chilli con carne

Serves 2
500g mince beef
1 clove of garlic, crushed
1 tsp dried chilli flakes (optional)
1 onion, chopped
1 red pepper, chopped
1 yellow pepper, chopped
1 large courgette, chopped
About 10 mushrooms, chopped
2 tins of chopped tomatoes
2 tins kidney beans in chilli sauce
Tablespoon olive oil
Worcestershire sauce
Salt and Pepper

Put the oil, garlic and onion into a large saucepan or wok and cook over a medium-high heat until the onion goes clear. Add the peppers and the chilli flakes and cook until the pepper is softened. Add the mince and brown until cooked through. Add the courgette and cook for another 4-5 minutes. Add the mushrooms and a good splash of Worcestershire sauce and cook for a further 2-3 minutes, making sure everything is mixed thoroughly. Add the tins of tomatoes and beans, mix thoroughly again and simmer until the beans are cooked through. Next, taste and adjust the seasoning as necessary, and serve hot, either alone or over rice.

Spaghetti Bolognese

Serves 2

500g minced beef

1 clove of garlic, crushed

Tablespoon olive oil

Salt and Pepper

1 onion, chopped

1 jar Bolognese sauce

Worcestershire sauce

Grated parmesan or cheddar cheese

For the Bolognese:
Put the oil, garlic and onion in bottom of saucepan over a medium/high heat and gently fry until the onion goes clear. Add the mince in and cook until browned. Once the mince is cooked through, add the Bolognese sauce and season with a good splash of Worcestershire sauce and a pinch of salt and pepper. Simmer over a low heat for 30 minutes to 1 hour, stirring occasionally.

For the Spaghetti:
Get a large saucepan of water, bring to the boil and add a pinch of salt. Add the spaghetti and cook as directed on packet, usually 10 minutes. Once cooked, drain the spaghetti. (Try to time it so that the spaghetti and bolognese are cooked at about the same time) Place spaghetti in bowls and top with bolognese sauce. Sprinkle with grated parmesan or cheddar cheese.

Burgers

There is a whole world of difference between a homemade and an internationally sold fast food burger. One is full of E-numbers, hydrogenated fats and excess salt, the whole thing makes you feels like you've swallowed a cannonball hours after eating, whereas the homemade burger is satisfying, wholesome and delicious to eat.

Serves 4 – You'll need to make four for all your new friends that you will acquired when word gets out on the quality of these burgers.

500 grams of the best quality minced meat your butcher can provide.

1 onion peeled and finely chopped

50 grams of breadcrumbs

1 tablespoon of French mustard

Worcestershire sauce

A touch of Tabasco

1 egg

1 clove of garlic

Dash of

Salt and pepper to taste

Put all the ingredients into a bowl and mix thoroughly. Allow to rest for 30 minutes in the fridge. Take out and shape into four burgers. Grill for about 4- 5 minutes on a medium grill on each side. Or fry in oil, turning once, for about 4 - 5 minutes on each side, or until they are golden brown.
Best served on burger buns with your favourite relishes.

Chicken coq-au-vin (Casserole chicken)

Strictly a French dish but has been adapted by the British very successfully. This meal will stand against any meal prepared by any chef, in any restaurant, at any price, in the world!

Serves 4

4 pieces of chicken breast, chop into cubes
a good quality packet mix for the sauce
(Colmans is to be recommended!)
OR
½ pint or ¼ litre of chicken stock
1 tablespoon of tomato puree
Very small glass of red wine
Small shallots chopped
Pinch of mixed herbs

To use the packet follow their cooking instructions **OR** start with the stock and add all of the other ingredients into a casserole dish and cook on 180° or gas mark 4 for 60-75 minutes. Serve with potatoes and seasonal vegetables.

Risotto

Serves 2

300g Arborio Rice
1 litre of hot chicken or vegetable stock
4 tablespoons butter
1 tablespoon olive oil
1 onion, chopped
2 cloves of garlic, chopped
2 sticks of celery, chopped
30ml white wine (optional)
Parmesan cheese

(You can also add a range of ingredients to make your risotto more exciting, for example other vegetables, bacon, chicken or herbs)

Heat the olive oil and half of the butter in a saucepan. Once the butter has melted add the onion, garlic and celery and sweat for five minutes until tender. Add in the rice and ensure all of the grains are coated in the fat. Continue to cook until the rice becomes slightly translucent. (Keep the rice moving in the pan to prevent it from sticking, the rice should be making sizzling sounds). Add the white wine and continue to cook until it is all absorbed. Next slowly add the stock, a ladleful at a time, allowing the rice to absorb the stock until all of the stock has been incorporated.

After 20 minutes or so, the rice should be cooked. At this point remove from the heat and stir in the remaining butter and grated parmesan. Serve immediately.

Beef stew

Serves 2

250 grams good stewing steak
1 onion, finely chopped
1 crushed clove of garlic
20 grams flour
½ litre beef stock (dissolve 1 stock cube in ½ litre water)
2 medium sized peeled and chopped carrots
2 tablespoons of olive oil
Optional salt to taste
Pepper to taste

Cut the meat into small pieces and roll them in some of the flour with salt and pepper. Heat the oil in a pan. Brown the meat on both sides.
Take the meat and put to one side.
In the same pan fry the onions and garlic for 5 minutes.
Put the rest of the flour in the pan and fry gently. Add the stock and boil until everything thickens. Add the carrots and steak then put into casserole dish. Bake on gas mark 4 or 180° for approximately 1 ½ hours.
Serve with creamy mashed potatoes and garden peas.

Corned beef hash

Corned beef hash was the staple diet for people in the last great war but then became very, very unfashionable, but made properly, is a wonderful satisfying meal and so easy to prepare and cook. Even the poorest cook cannot make a mess of this meal.

Serves 2

1 tin of corned beef
Large onion, peeled and chopped
4-5 large potatoes, peeled and diced
Milk
Butter
2 tablespoons of olive oil

Place the potatoes in a saucepan of boiling salted water; boil until tender, about 10-15 minutes.
Drain and mash with a little butter and milk.
Heat the oil in a large pan and fry the onions for about 5 minutes until golden brown.
Open the tin of corned beef chop into small pieces and add to the onion.
Heat the beef thoroughly then ad the mashed potato.
Fry until the potato is crispy but not burnt!

Buying A Car

If you buy a car either privately from an auction or a dealer and you have problems with your new vehicle you must take it back to the seller straight away. If you then have problems with the seller you are able to get more advice from your local trading standards service.

Buying a car privately:

It may be cheaper to buy a car privately but doing so will leave you with hardly any legal rights, in many situations the car is described as something it is not. Knowing whom you are buying the car from and where they live is therefore very important, you should also inspect the vehicle at the sellers home also taking a good mechanic with you or someone who is familiar with cars if possible.

It is not a good idea to buy a car from a car park or motorway service or any other general public place; this makes it harder to contact the seller should you have problems with the car.

If you have bought your car and it breaks down half way home you may not have any legal rights whatsoever unless for example it was described as – just passed MOT – when there is really no way that it could have. Be aware also that some local advertisements say they are private sellers when really they are dealers trying to sell as private to avoid their legal obligations.

Buying from a dealer:

The law says that when you buy a car from a dealer it should be: Of satisfactory quality, as described and fit for purpose. If you see some faults when looking at your new car and the dealer has not firstly pointed these out to you then it is not really of satisfactory quality.

Of course if you're looking at second hand cars there is bound to be faults somewhere as you would expect of a sign of previous use.

The dealer should tell you about the history of the car – this means as described – he will tell you about the previous owners, if he says the car has had one careful owner it should not turn out to have had several.

When you tell your dealer exactly what you want from your new car he should find you something that fits this purpose.

If these points are not met or you have problems with your car you may have the right to take it back if you do this straight away and get your money back. Once you have decided the car is not what you asked for or is not fit for purpose you must stop using it immediately and tell the dealer. If the dealer will not take back the car or give you a refund it is then up to you to prove your case. You will need to get an independent assessment of vehicle and sue for damages. However if you choose to do repairs on the car you can insist the dealer gives you other transport or pays for your travel while your new car is being repaired.

Test drive tips:

If you can, try and take the car for a 24-hour test drive instead of driving the dealer's route so you can see how the car copes with the kind of journeys you actually make. Alternatively, if you can't get a 24-hour test drive, ask to drive your own route, testing the car on all types of roads.

Check the seat positions, not only for you, but also for anyone else that will be driving the car. There is no point buying a car only you can drive if its for more drivers, so make sure everyone will be comfortable.

See how much fuel you use – don't just trust the fuel consumption figures shown to you.

Buying from a car auction:

Firstly, be careful when going to auctions, especially if it is your first time. You can find some great bargains but it is quite risky and the usual legal rights may not apply if a 'disclaimer' is on the vehicle eg: 'sold as seen'. You may feel better if you go to these auctions several times before you make a decision on a car, you will get used to the atmosphere of the auction and observe the way the place works, you can also get used to some of the terms used such as 'direct cars' which are ex-company cars. If you do not know much about cars it will be helpful for you to take along someone who does. If you really want a bargain it is important to stay with your price and not be tempted to bid higher.

It is recommended to buy cars from auction that are between 2-5 years old. Always check for fuel service history and check that the auction can be sure the car you want is not stolen as this can happen. It is on your best interest to contact the RAC to get your car 'H.P.I'd.' This gives you information as to whether your car has been in an accident, whether there's any finance owed on it, whether its been stolen or recovered, whether its been involved in an insurance total lost. It's basically a full check of the vehicle's history. It will cost you approximately 35/40 pounds.

Car Maintenance

Screenwash

- Check and top up regularly – it's a legal requirement that it is in good working order
- Use a good screen wash through summer and winter. Washing up liquid mixed with water is alright as a cheap alternative as long as you use a lot of water but can clog up so a specialist product is recommended

Wipers

- Wiper blades wear down over time and smear the windscreen if they become warn
- Replace them at least once a year for best performance. You can fit them yourself as they are easy to fit. If you can't see you can't drive it's illegal

Lights

- Check all lights weekly. Don't forget indicators, brake and fog lights. Spare bulbs should always be carried in the car
- Clean lights regularly

Toolkit

- Make sure you know where your car's toolkit is – it should have a jack and wheel removal kit at least
- Familiarise yourself with the jacking points used to lift the car safely
- A blanket to lie on and a set of overalls can be invaluable in times of a breakdown
- Copies of your driving licence, MOT and Insurance kept locked in the boot can save you a lot of time in case of being stopped by the police or if you are involved in an accident

You never know what time of the year you break down; it could be in the depth of winter even something like an old sweater could be invaluable.

The only time you will appreciate these points is when you breakdown – and you will take my word for it.

TYRE PRESSURE

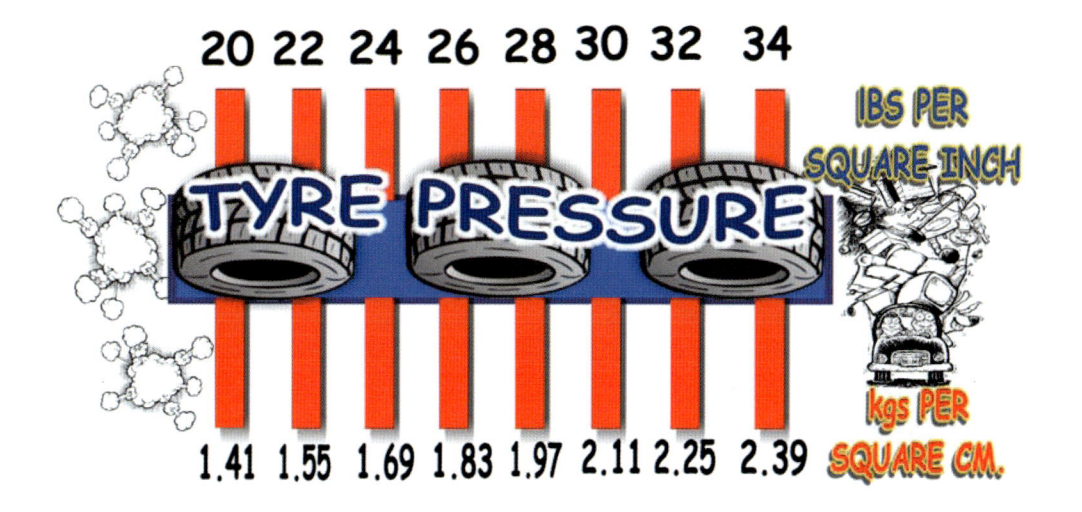

20 22 24 26 28 30 32 34 — lbs per square inch

1.41 1.55 1.69 1.83 1.97 2.11 2.25 2.39 — kgs per square cm.

> **1966 – England's Greatest Year of Football**
>
> **Can also be used as an easy way to remember the difference between Celsius and Fahrenheit.**

19° Celsius is roughly equal to 66° Fahrenheit

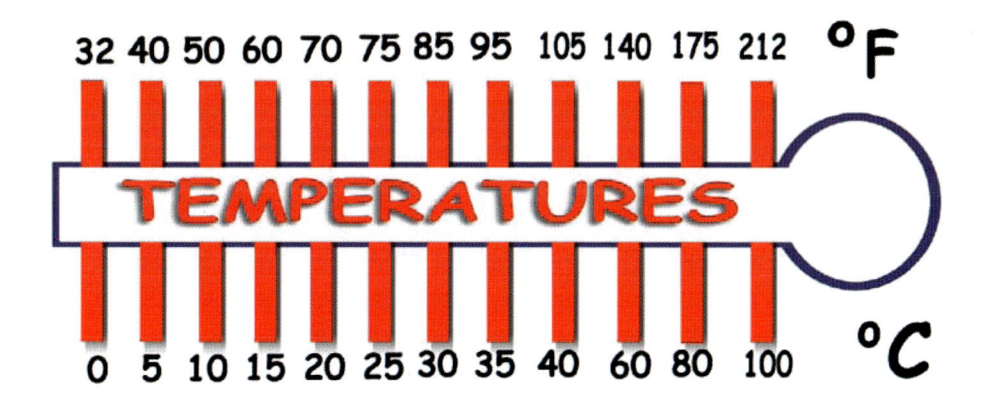

TEMPERATURES

°F: 32 40 50 60 70 75 85 95 105 140 175 212

°C: 0 5 10 15 20 25 30 35 40 60 80 100

DRIVING

You are not legally allowed to drive a car until you are 17 unless you get disability living allowance at the higher rate. At 16 you can ride a moped and you must be 21 to drive medium or large sized vehicles like mini buses or buses.

Before you start driving a vehicle you must check if it is roadworthy. If it is 3 or more years old it must have an MOT certificate to be roadworthy and therefore legal to drive. It must also have a tax disk that is not out of date if it is less than 30 years old to be legal to drive. You must also have insurance to drive the vehicle and a valid driving licence (or provisional licence, L-Plates attached to the car and a supervisor who will sit in the passenger seat who is at least 21 with at least 3 years driving experience on a full licence and who is insured to drive the vehicle).

- If you do not have an MOT certificate you can get one by making an appointment at a garage to have your car MOT'd (the police will only let you off if you are pulled over with no MOT certificate if you are driving the car directly to the garage to have an MOT). Having an MOT done can be expensive as there can be things that need to be done to your car in order to make it roadworthy and be given an MOT certificate.

- To get your vehicle taxed you will need a form from your local post office. Road tax for a normal car costs about £110 for one year. Remember it is illegal to have your car on the road even if it is parked on the street if it has not been taxed.

- Car insurance can be provided by any number of companies. Generally it is significantly more expensive for persons under 25 and can be even more expensive for men with some companies due to research which shows statistically men have more accidents than women. Some companies have now been set up that will only insure women drivers so if you are a man you cannot use these however if you are a woman they could work out cheaper. Vehicle power, risk assessment of the area the car is left in, value of the car and criminal convictions are all factors that will affect how much the insurance will be.

- To get car insurance you will need to either telephone around insurance companies to get a quote (this involves answering a lot of questions) or get quotes online from some companies. It is best to compare the quotes you are given and go with the cheapest one. You will have to pay either monthly or yearly though yearly can work out cheaper if you can afford the payment in full.
- To apply for a provisional driving licence if you do not already have one you will need to fill out and send (along with a cheque) a D1 form that you can get from your local post office and then your licence will be posted to you at the address you provide on the form. If you have passed your driving test you can apply for a full driving licence. This will happen immediately after you pass.

Learning to Drive

To learn to drive you have to have someone who is 21 has been driving on a full licence for at least three years and who has a full licence sat in the front passenger seat to tell you what to do. You have to also have what are called 'L plates' attached to the front and back of your vehicle either in the corner of your windscreen (so it doesn't block your view) or attached to the outside of the car somewhere visible. L plates should look like the picture above – basically just a big red letter L on a white background!

Taking a Theory Test

Nowadays you have to pass what is known as a 'theory test' before you can take an actual driving test. To apply for this visit: www.dvla.gov.uk. You will have to answer 35 questions that are to do with driving and get at least 30 of them right. You also have to take what is called a 'Hazard Perception Test' as part of the 'Theory Test'. This is where you will have to watch about 15 thirty second long video clips and click the mouse any time you see something you think could be a hazard to the driver of the car it is filmed from. You can't just click away like mad or the machine will detect that you are cheating. Also if you try clicking every few seconds just to try your luck it will do the same thing! Once you have had enough driving experience this test should be easy for you but if you are not feeling so confident you could try practice tests and tuition which you can buy on a CD from most good bookshops. There is also a practice theory test on the Driving Standards Agency website. www.dsa.gov.uk

My Top 10 Countries To Visit

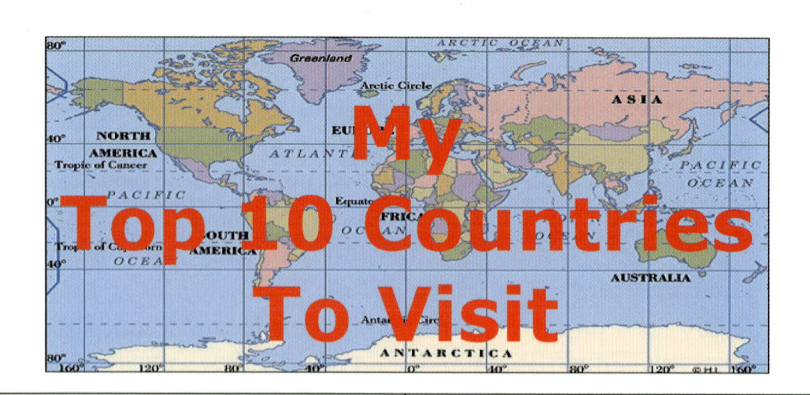

Country:	Country:
Date Visited:	Date Visited:
Country:	Country:
Date Visited:	Date Visited:
Country:	Country:
Date Visited:	Date Visited:
Country:	Country:
Date Visited:	Date Visited:
Country:	Country:
Date Visited:	Date Visited:

Applying for/Renewing your passport

You will need to make an appointment at a Passport Office which can take up to a week. There are only seven of these in the U.K.:
Belfast, Durham, Glasgow, Liverpool, London, Newport and Peterborough.

You will need to go to the office on the day your appointment is and be at least 10 minutes early.

When you go to the passport office you will need to bring the expired passport and a completed renewal form which you will need to ask for from your local post office. If you have any problems with this form the post office can help you as well as the passport office officials at the passport office.

There is usually a queue for passports and you will have to go through a metal detector and possibly be searched. The passport officer at the desk will give you a number and ask you to wait in the seating area. When your number is called out you will be told to go to a counter where another passport officer will take your expired passport, your completed forms and your payment of either for Premium (same day) Service (to get your passport in four hours or less from the same passport), or for First Track Service (to get your passport sent to your house within a week).

From the 5th October 2006, the fees for British passports were increased, and prices are now as follows:

Standard	Guaranteed same day (renewals only)	Guaranteed one week service
Adult £66	Adult £108	Adult £91
Child £45	Child £93	Child £80

Another way to renew your passport is to send off your form and expired or soon to expire passport in the post. It is necessary to send this recorded delivery in case your passport is stolen. Sending your passport in the post will take considerably longer for it to arrive back (possibly even a month and even then this is not guaranteed) so it is not a suitable method if you are going to leave the country soon.

What to do if you have lost/ had your passport stolen or damaged

Again you will need to make an appointment at your nearest passport office but you cannot get the premium same day service. You will also need to fill in and take with you (or send off in the post if you wish) an <mark>LS01 form</mark> from your local post office as well as. This form cancels your lost/stolen/damaged passport so you can get a new one.

Remember: You will need to telephone before you go to book a set time for someone to see you at a passport office.

<mark>Please note:</mark> to apply for a British Passport you must be at least 16 and be either:

- A British Citizen
- A British Dependent Territories Citizen
- A British Overseas Citizen
- A British Subject

It will also be expected of you to produce a photograph of yourself (passport size) which needs to be signed by someone over 18 if it is your first passport. You will also need to show that you are British. You can show this by taking with you as many other forms of I.D. (Identification) as possible. Other forms of Identification include:

- Birth Certificates
- Driving Licence
- Medical Card
- National Insurance Card
- Benefit Book

When your passport arrives or you are given it at a Passport Office make sure that the details on it are correct and make a note of them in case it is ever stolen.

If you have any more queries, contact the **Passport Advice line** on: **0870 521 0410**

This national advice line provides a single point of contact for all telephone callers and is available 24 hours a day, 7 days a week to:

- Answer all straight forward enquiries;
- Make an appointment for you to call at one of our passport offices, should you need your passport in less than two weeks;
- Transfer calls to specialists at the Passport Service regional offices if your questions are complex and require a trained passport **examiner to** provide an answer.

MAIL

A big problem when leaving home is receiving mail to your new address. Whether you are going into a shared house or flat, you may be living in a shared house with other people where there is a chance your mail may go missing!

Whilst at times this could be just an inconvenience, (such as receiving flyers etc), other times it can be more serious such as cheques or money disappearing, severely hitting your purse.

Alternatively, loss of mail may be cause trouble and arguments within a shared household. It can cast a shadow and even make living there impossible.

This is a situation that can be resolved very easily.

You can arrange to collect your mail from the Post Office at a time that suits you. They will retain your mail at your local delivery office for you to collect at your own convenience, Monday to Saturday from 8.30 am until closing time.

And best of all this service is absolutely free!

FORWARDING MAIL TO YOUR NEW ADDRESS

The Royal Mail also offers a re-direction service. This will ensure your letters and parcels are successfully delivered to your new address.

To qualify for the service you must be living at the actual address the mail is being directed to. It is an offence to redirect mail without proper authority.

The cost for this service will depend on the length of redirection required and the number of surnames requesting the service at that address.

To obtain this service you will collect a form from the post office.

You will also be required to show some form of identification.

Once the form is completed and the fee paid, the post office will notify you in writing that the re-direction service is about to commence.

The post office will later write to you offering to extend the service approximately 2 weeks before your agreed redirection time has expired.

To take advantage of this service, visit your local or general post office.

HOW DO I MAIL COLLECT?

Just follow these simple steps;
- Complete an application form that is available from your local Post Office.
- Once completed, take the form to your local delivery office with appropriate identification.

Acceptable identification would be…

CHEQUE GUARANTEE, CREDIT OR DEBIT CARD.
BANK OR BUILDING SOCIETY BOOK.
PASSPORT (ANY NATIONALITY).
NATIONAL SAVINGS BOOK.
STORE ACCOUNT CARD (EMBOSSED, NOT A LOYALTY CARD).
2 RECENT UTILITY BILLS (THIS COUNTS AS ONE ITEM AND DOES NOT INCLUDE MOBILE PHONE BILLS OR STORE/CHARGE BILLS).
DRIVING LICENCE (IF A PHOTOCARD LICENCE, IT MUST BE ACCOMPANYED BY THE COUNTERPART DRIVING LICENCE-FORM D740, WHICH IS ISSUED WITH THE CARD).
COUNCIL TAX PAYMENT BOOK.
RECENT BANK/BUILDING SOCIETY STATEMENT.
COUNCIL RENT BOOK.
CREDIT CARD STATEMENT.

GOING ON HOLIDAY

If you are away from home for a while, make sure you don't leave obvious clues about your absence, such as a pile of mail on your doormat!
For a small nominal fee the Royal Mail also offer a "KEEPSAFE" service. This gives you peace of mind in the knowledge your mail is being looked after while you are away and delivered to you when you return.
To obtain this service merely obtain a form from your local Post Office and list your dates of absence. Ensure you give the Royal Mail at least five days notice.
You want to make sure that any important letters or valuable documents sent to you whilst you're away are kept in safe hands. Keepsafe gives you peace of mind that your mail is being looked after while you're away and

will be delivered to you in the next available delivery after the date you choose.

For only five pounds thirty five you'll get two weeks Keepsafe for everyone in your household.

You'll have enough to think about just before you go away so why not arrange your Keepsafe in good time before you go? They only need five working days notice.

How much does it cost?
    17 days = £5.70
    34 days = £9.10
    31 days = £11.40
    66 days = £17.15

ESSENTIAL TIPS FOR POSTING

There are different services available to you depending on the content, value and urgency of your mail. Choose the correct service to suit you.

All mail needs is the correct Postcode. If in doubt visit www.royalmail.com to use your Postcode finder.

Putting a return address on the reverse of your letter will ensure, in the unlikely event your letter cannot be delivered, it can at least be returned to you.

Essential tips for posting…

- There are different services available to you depending on the content, value and urgency of your mail. Choose the correct service to suit your needs.
- All mail needs to have a correct postcode
- Ensure you package your item so that the contents are adequately protected
- Putting a return address on the back of your item will ensure, if it cannot be delivered, we will return it to you
- If you are concerned that your mail has been lost, damaged or delayed, pick up a claim form (P58) from your local post office

Buying Goods

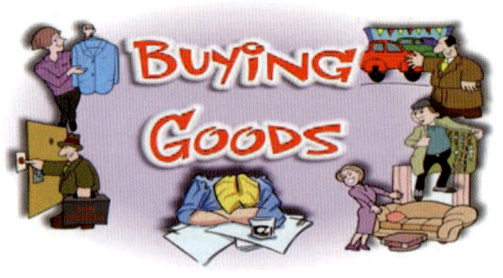

Due to youth and inexperience some people will try to take advantage of you. The experience that you gain through life will give you the confidence to not be brow-beaten. Right now you may be at your most vulnerable and when you get older you may be able to afford mistakes but not now, you must watch every penny carefully.

First and foremost: *Goods MUST be fit for the purpose they were intended for. This includes sale rate goods as long as the faults were pointed out.*

Deposits: *Do not leave a deposit unless you really have to; even then always leave as small a deposit as you possibly can.*

Receipts: *Always ask for a receipt whether using cash or cheque and keep it safe.*

How to Complain

There are many different situations that arise in daily life where you feel wronged and then you worry about how to complain. Most of us simply put up with the late delivery of something we have ordered or the faulty toaster, which works only one day a week and electrocutes us the rest of the time! Others are afraid to complain after trying in the past and getting nowhere. It is your right to complain if something is just not good enough for you…but there is a special way to complain, an art if you like and some ways work better than others.

There are no set rules of complaining and no guarantee it will always work. Sometimes it really will be like a battle and you will be angry and frustrated and want to scream and shout, especially when that person behind the desk or at the end of the phone doesn't seem to be listening.

However, by doing this you will simply make that person angry too and therefore a resolution will take longer to appear. If the complaint is about goods you have bought, it is important to stop using them straight away.

Many people continue to use their goods until the day they take them back but this can make a refund or replacement impossible.

If the complaint is not straightforward eg: a lot of minor problems about a product or situation, the best thing to do is make a note of all the points writing them down as they occur. This applies with problems for example with trade work/building work. Decide how you want to complain- by phone, letter, in person, then get the name of the person who deals with the complaints and also find out the name of the person they report to. This way if nothing seems to happen with your complaint you can follow it up.

To get the names you need to ring the organisation and just say you are making a complaint, you do not need to give them any details.

Remember: Those complainers who, in the end, get what they want manage to keep their cool and be assertive at the same time and are never aggressive. This may take some practice and it may be hard to imagine when your anger is boiling inside to remember your humour…but this is important too.

The person you are dealing with is only doing their job, even if they are doing it badly.

When making your complaint give them a deadline and keep a record of each response you get from them, even if it is not written down eg: via telephone/message. If your first complaint does not get a response within a few weeks time then you should send another letter by recorded delivery. This time tell them if no response is received that you will take legal action.

KEEP A COPY OF ALL CORRESPONDENCE.

Trading Standards

Trading Standards offices can help you to complain against shops and other traders who may try and rip you off. They will investigate complaints about goods, prices and can even stop dangerous goods from being sold. The law says if you buy a faulty item that was not pointed out to you as faulty you deserve a full refund as long as you complain quickly enough! You could also be offered a replacement or a repair but this is your choice. For more information about your shopping rights you could contact:

- Office of Fair Trading (OFT) 08457 224 499
- The Financial Ombudsman 0845 0801 800
- Banking Code Service Standards Board 020 7661 9694

CITIZENS ADVICE
the charity for your community

You'll find them in your local phone book. If you have a problem…ring them NOW!

ABOUT CARE ADVICE

The Citizen's Advice Bureau is an independent organisation that provides free, confidential and impartial advice from over 3,500 locations. These locations include bureau offices, G.P. surgeries, hospitals, colleges, prisons and Courts. It can even include home visits.

Advice is available face to face or through home visit or e-mail. Their advice can assist people in such areas as debt, receiving benefits, housing, legal matters, discrimination, employment, immigration and consumer issues to name but a few.

THE PRINCIPLES OF C.A.B. ADVICE

INDEPENDENT
They will always act in the interest of their client, without influence from any outside party.

IMPARTIAL
They do not judge clients or make assumptions about them. Everyone is treated equally.

CONFIDENTIAL
No information is passed to any other party unless their client requests it or gives their permission to do so.

FREE
Their service is totally free.

Alcohol Abuse:	020 7833 0022
Childline:	0800 11 11
NSPCC Child Protection Helpline:	0800 800 500
Citizens Advice Bureau:	0161 831 9190
Victim Support:	020 7735 9166
National Debtline:	08088 084 000
Drugs-Release Emergency services:	020 7729 9904
Drugs-Turning Point:	020 7702 2300
Drugs-Resolve:	0808 800 2345

(information and support about solvent and volatile substance abuse issues)

Drugs-Talk to Frank: 0800 77 66 00
(information about drugs for people who use them, their friends, families and colleagues)

Gingerbread: 020 7488 9300
(provides lone parents with support and advice)

Relate: 08702 40 4246/ 0845 130 40 10
(relationship counseling and marriage guidance)

National council for One Parent Families: 080 88 00 2222
(local parent link education and support groups)

HELP!!!
Is only a 📞 call away

British Pregnancy Advisory Service:	01256 359 720
National Childbirth Trust:	0870 444 8707
Association for Postnatal Illness:	02073 860 868
Gamblers Anonymous (24 hour):	0161 976 5000
Shelter *(the National Campaign for Homeless People):*	02075 05 2000
Missing Persons:	0800 700 740

(CONFIDENTIAL helpline for those who have left home/run away to send a message home and to get confidential help and advice)

Missing persons Bureau Helpline:	020839 24545
The Salvation Army Family Tracing Service:	02073 674747
Samaritans(emergency 24hour line):	08457 909090
Smokers Quitline:	0800 00 22 00
Get connected:	*0808 808 4994*

(finds young people the best help whatever the problem

Asian Child Protection line: 0800 096 7719

GIVING BLOOD

Helping others is the greatest way to help yourself. To do something really amazing why not give blood?
Your blood donation could help people during accident and emergency transfusions, during childbirth, during heart surgery, even someone undergoing cancer treatment.
Being a blood donor gives us the great satisfaction of realising our own problems can easily be put into perspective and helps are own feelings of lethargy or depression!

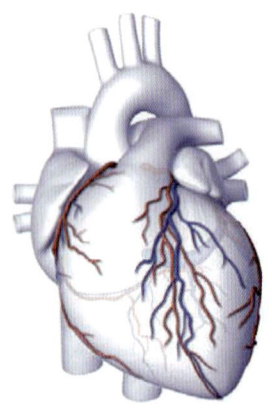

Hospitals need around 10,000 blood donations every single day, not just for accidents and emergencies but also for so many other things and demands for blood are always rising. All of us are dependant on kind and selfless individuals to give their blood – people like you and me. If you are in good health aged between 17-60 you can give blood, it is so easy to do something amazing and every kind of blood is desperately needed not just rare ones, the more common the blood type, the more of it is needed.
To give your blood for the first time will take about an hour, you will be asked routine questions about your health then a drop of blood taken from your finger will be checked for things like anaemia then if all is well a donation will be taken.

It is all painless, and most people hardly even feel a thing. A donation of about ¾ pint of blood will be collected and after a short rest with a cup of tea and biscuits you will be ready to go.

IT'S AS SIMPLE AS THAT!

Taking an hour out of your busy schedule to help to save a life, a life you know, a life you don't know, it doesn't matter, you will know that you have given the one thing you can to help that someone who needs you the most.
When contacted the national blood service will inform you of the next donation session held in your area: www.blood.co.uk or call 0845 7711 711

On Behalf of the people whose lives you are going to save:

A Heartfelt Thank You

Organ Donation - Give the gift of life

One of the most miraculous achievements of modern medicine is organ donation, and you can very easily become part of the miracle.

One donor can give life to several people and restore the sight of two more. The more people who pledge to donate their organs after their death, the more people stand to benefit. By choosing to join the NHS Organ Donor Register, you can help to make sure life goes on.

When you register it is important that you tell those closest to you about your decision, even if your name is on the register the person closest to you in life will be asked to confirm that you had not changed your mind. Putting your name on the register demonstrates your consent to the use of your organs for transplantation.

To decide whether or not you wish to become a donor after you have died is something very personal and it is important that everyone makes their own decision.

Organ donation is the gift of an organ to help someone who needs a transplant. The generosity of donors and their families enables nearly 3,000 people in the UK every year to take on a new lease of life. In addition, thousands of people have their sight restored by donated corneas. In the United Kingdom organs from potential donors can only be used if that is their wish. Putting your name on the NHS Organ Donor Register and carrying a card makes it easy for the NHS to establish your wishes. There is no cost whatsoever related to the donation of your organs, as the entire cost is bourn by the National Health Service.

Please, please, please become part of this modern miracle. The satisfaction you will gain will be enormous and if you can possibly encourage your friends to do the same, please do so.

For more information contact:
0845 60 60 400

THE SALVATION ARMY

"Wherever people need our love...we have to be there"

For many lonely and unhappy people the Salvation Army will be their only friend.
When people are homeless, the Salvation Army are there to offer support and practical help such as food and shelter.

They also care for the elderly who are alone and protect children when neglected or abused.
In fact whatever problem you experience, the Salvation Army are there to support.

The Salvation Army was founded by William Booth and his wife Catherine. In 1865 he and his wife formed an evangelical group dedicated to preaching amongst the "unchurched" people living amidst the appalling poverty in the East End of London.
Booth's ministry recognized the requirement of material, emotional and spiritual needs.
In addition to preaching the gospel of Jesus Christ, Booth became involved in the feeding and shelter of the hungry and homeless as well as the rehabilitation of alcoholics.

William Booth's philosophies formed the corner stone of the Social Services we know today. Their work has expanded over the last century to include disaster relief services, services for the aging, AIDS education and residential services and shelters for women and children subjected to domestic violence. Also, they offer family and career counselling as well as abuse rehabilitation.
More than 30,000,000 people each year are helped through one of the services provided by the Salvation Army.

If you wish to contact the Salvation Army they can be located in your local phone directory, or alternatively through their website address at: www.salvationarmy.org.uk.
Alternatively you can locate them through your local Yellow Pages or Thompson Local Directory.

SAMARITANS

A marvellous organisation in your hour of need is called the Samaritans. You can contact the Samaritans when you are having a troubling time and you need someone to talk to about it.

They are contactable on **08457 909090** and are available to you 24 hours a day.
There are also local numbers you can call and their website address is: www.samaritans.co.uk

Alternatively you can locate them through your local Yellow Pages or Thompson Local Directory.
Perhaps you prefer to talk to someone who is impartial and somebody that you do not know. Somebody who will not be judgemental yet can see the situation clearly and without a biased mind.
That is exactly what the Samaritans are.

They are trained to listen without prejudice to whatever you have to say. All people in the Samaritans are volunteers and offer their time and expertise freely.

They can listen sympathetically and offer options that you could take in a bad situation that perhaps you had not considered.
They can also offer coping strategies so you can deal with whatever problems you have in your life.
They are totally confidential, which means anything you tell them remains between you and the person confided in.

The only exceptions of where confidentiality may be broken is if…

- *You attack them.*
- *You deliberately attempt to prevent other people from using their service.*
- *They receive a Court order forcing them to divulge information.*

They call an ambulance because you are in a state of mind where you are unable to make rational decisions yourself.

VOLUNTEERING FOR THE SAMARITANS

If you feel you would like to become a volunteer for the Samaritans you can call them on : 08705 627282.

They can tell you when and where they are holding training sessions for new volunteers.

Alternatively, you can contact their website: www.samaritans.co.uk .

Volunteers find being a Samaritan rewarding for so many reasons, from improving communication skills to feeling of satisfaction through knowing they have helped another person in need.

For to be free is not merely to cast off one's chains, but to live in a way that respects and enhances the freedom of others.

Nelson Mandela 1995

St John's Ambulance

St John's Ambulance is the UK's leading First Aid, Transport and Care charity.
Their vision is that:

'Everyone who needs it should receive First Aid from those around them. No-one should suffer for the lack of trained First-Aiders.'

As a result, St John's Ambulance
- Offers First Aid training for volunteers of all ages
- Ensures public events (both large and small) have First Aid cover so that they can take place safely
- Provides caring services within the community through multiple schemes, offering support for young people, young carers, the elderly, the homeless and many more.

Volunteering

Not only is volunteering with St John's an opportunity to learn First Aid – it's also a good way of developing new skills, gaining new experiences and meeting new people. And you'll not only be changing your life, you'll be helping other people's too!

You can volunteer from at any age, with age groups divided into the following programmes
- Badgers – Ages 5 - 10
- Cadets – Ages 10 – 18
- Links (Student wing) – Ages 16 - 25

So, if you've been volunteering with St John's Ambulance in the Cadets programme, but are now over 18 moving into higher education, there is no reason for you to stop!

The LINKS programme allows volunteers in higher education to continue volunteering whilst studying, continues with their training, and is flexible, allowing you to give as much time as you wish.

There are also many volunteering opportunities for adults in various roles. To become a volunteer, you can register your interest by calling on 08700 104950 or you can register online at:

www.sja.org.uk/volunteering/register

Political Help

We live in a 'Democracy'. This means that everyone's views are taken into consideration. When a vote is held it is up to you to vote on what you think is best otherwise someone else will choose for you!

A great source of help is your local counsellor or MP. They are very much under used as a source of information, but the majority of them in-spite of popular belief are in the business of helping people. Most local counsellors hold, what is known as surgeries at least once a month, when they will only be too pleased to discuss any local problems with you. For instance if you have any problems with roads, schools or dustbin collection services. They have to act on the interests of the majority of their constituents or they will be voted out of their jobs.

Members of Parliament (MP's) are basically the same thing except they are in charge of a larger area and are in what is called a 'Party'. A 'Party' is a group of people with the same set of views on issues that affect the country such as 'Tax', 'Transport' or 'The Euro'. MP's are also part of what is called the 'House of Commons', this is where the 659 MP's meet to discuss the running of the country. The 'Party' with the most MP's is the Government as it is the most popular party. The only drawback is they mainly stick to the party line on most issues, but are very concerned about local issues if it could get them re-elected at the next election.
The other MP's are known as the opposition, and are called 'backbenchers', however they still represent your views in parliament and cannot be disregarded.

192

The Prime Minister is the head of the most popular party. He has what is called 'The Cabinet' to help him. They meet to discuss decisions in what is called a 'Cabinet Meeting' and when they have come to a decision the Members of the Cabinet support the decision publicly.

The Monarchy doesn't really have any say over how the country is run anymore, although it used to. This is a family that used to have all the power over all the other families in the country and would be in charge of the army as well as the law. The sons or daughters of the family would be called princesses and princes and the mum and dad were the king and queen. Usually the eldest son would become the next king who would have control over the country and it would be passed on like that. The family is known as the 'Royal Family'. We still have a Royal Family and at the head of this at the minute is the Queen. Nowadays she doesn't have control over the country though she does have duties that are informal. Mainly she helps to raise money for the country with her fame though she does have the right to give her opinion to the government about matters concerning the country.

The House of Commons is sometimes known as the 'Lower House' and is the place where MP's meet to discuss decisions the Government has made by making reports.

The House of Lords is made up of people that aren't elected so they have less power and limited effect on how the country is run.

Clothing Sizes

Clothing sizes vary depending on where they were made. Sizing usually falls under British sizing, American sizing and Continental sizing. Size equivalents are also approximate, but the guides below should give you an idea of what a British size is roughly equivalent to in America etc.

Men's suits and coats

British	38	40	42	44	46	48
American	38	40	42	44	46	48
Continental	48	50	52	54	56	58

Men's shirts

British	14 ½	15	15 ½	16	16 ½	17
American	14 ½	15	15 ½	16	16 ½	17
Continental	37	38	39/40	41	42	43

Men's shoes

British	7	7 ½	8 ½	9 ½	10 ½	11
American	8	8 ½	9 ½	10 ½	11 ½	12
Continental	41	42	43	44	45	46

Women's dresses and suits

British	8	10	12	14	16	18
American	6	8	10	12	14	16
Continental	36	38	40	42	44	46

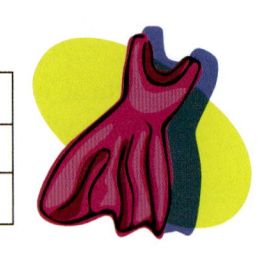

Women's shoes

British	4 ½	5	5 ½	6	6 ½	7
American	6	6 ½	7	7 ½	8	8 ½
Continental	38	38	39	39	40	41

WASHING

To keep your clothes lasting long. It is important to follow the instructions given on the label. Alternatively, below is a guide to general information on washing and drying garments.

Maximum temperature 60°C.
Normal spin cycle.

Maximum spin cycle 60°C.
Slow spin cycle.

Maximum temperature 40°C.
Normal spin cycle.

Maximum temperature 40°C.
Slow spin cycle.

Maximum temperature 30°C.
Slow spin cycle. (If you do not have this symbol on your washing machine it is wise to hand wash your garment.)

Dissolve the detergent carefully in the water (35°C – 40°C) before you add the garment. Avoid soaking. Squeeze the garment from the water, don't rub or wring.

Rinse carefully.

Do not wash.

Dry clean with regular dry cleaning fluids.

Do not dry clean.
No stain removal with solvents.

DRYING

To maintain the garment's original look it is important to notice the symbol that indicates whether it should be tumble dried or not. NEVER risk tumble-drying garments that are not manufactured for tumble-drying! If you choose to dry your garments in an airing cupboard you must make certain that the temperature does not exceed the temperature quoted on the garment label. Drying at room temperature is the best thing for *any* garment.

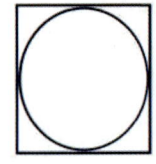

Tumble dry at normal temperature settings Maximum temperature 60°C.

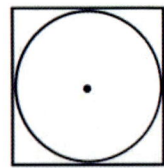

Tumble dry at lower a temperature setting. Maximum temperature 45°C.

No tumble dry

Sort garments by colour and given washing temperatures. Always wash similar colours together, i.e. whites. Mixing colours can cause the coloured dye to run, especially if washed at a higher temperature.

Detergent

Do not use too much! Extra detergent will not give better results.
The excess may remain and cause skin irritation. Measure out the detergent as per instructions on the packet.
If you know that your water in your area is hard then use more detergent. Alternatively if your area has softer water then use less detergent.
If uncertain contact your local water authority.

How to be Energy Efficient

Whilst you were living at home, you probably saw little point in being energy efficient, and may even have found your parents' constant nagging to turn off the lights every time you left a room irritating.

However, now that the electricity bill has your name on it, being more careful about how much power you use will help keep your bills down.

Making your home Energy Efficient

Whilst it may seem unlikely, it is often the little things that bump up your energy bills, such as leaving phone chargers plugged in and turned on with no phone attached, or leaving your TV on standby. Here are some easy ways to cut down on wasted power.

Insulation – Making sure your home has loft and cavity wall insulation may seem unrelated to your electricity usage, but a well insulated home cuts down on the amount of heating you will need.

Washing Clothes – Avoid drying clothes on radiators, and always use the cycle most suited to your washing load when using the washing machine. Most machines will have an economy cycle that may be cheaper to use.

Lights – Low energy light bulbs last much longer than regular bulbs and use up to 80% less electricity.

Heating – Turning your heating down by as little as 1°C can save you up to 10% on your heating bill.

Switch off – Turn off lights you're not using and don't leave appliances switched on if you are not using them (e.g. turn off the TV properly; don't just leave it on stand-by).

Dishwashing – Always try to run a dishwasher cycle with a full load.

Pest Control

Rats

The **Common Rat** is the most abundant widespread species. It typically has brownish fur on its back and grey underneath its belly, but colour can vary from white to black. Adult body length is 200-270mm with a tail length of 160-200mm.
They have small eyes, a rounded snout and are truly omnivorous.
The eat 25-30g of food a day and need to drink water regularly. They live in any situation that provides food, water and shelter, including sewers.
For rats, fully trained Pest Control Officers will carry out a survey and then place poison bat in the most appropriate locations. Follow up visits will be made to ensure the success of the treatment and to remove any remains of poison bait on completion.

Mice

The **House Mouse** is a common domestic pest, which, upon entering properties, will nest in roof spaces, under floors, in partitions, and any void or ducting that will allow them harbourage. Mice are mainly active at night and will range over small areas where food is plentiful. They are less dependent on water than rats and will normally obtain sufficient moisture from their food.

Mice, like rats, are a major hazard to health. They are responsible for the spread of many diseases, some of which can be fatal to man. They eat food which may be intended for human consumption and contaminate much more with their urine, droppings and fur. Particularly mice can cause structural damage to property by gnawing on electrical wiring, pipes, insulation and household items. Mice will gnaw their way through wood to gain access to sources of food.

For mice there are several options, obviously the more you do the more chance of eradicating the infestation. Break back traps baited with cereal or biscuit can be used, placed next to walls where mice tend to travel. Also mouse poison can be bought fairly easily from hardware stores and garden centres. When using poisonous substances, always read the label and follow instructions, especially regarding disposal of dead bodies.

Professional help should be sought when dealing with infestations of mice or rats. They are particularly difficult to control because of the rate at which they breed. By law, sightings of rats should be reported to your Local Authority. They are social creatures and, with an average litter of nine, that one sighting means you have only seen the tip of the iceberg!

Insects

Cockroaches are nocturnal and spend the day hiding in cracks and crevices around such areas as sinks, drains, cookers, skirting boards, service ducts and fridge motor compartments. The average adult cockroach is about half an inch long and smaller when young. It has a flattened oval shape and long feelers. One of the most common types is the German cockroach that is light brown with two black stripes behind its head. This type of roach is more abundant than the Oriental cockroach. They eat almost any kind of food, as well as household items, like glue, leather and bookbinding's.
Cockroaches are an important health problem because they smell bad, put germs in our food and bring sickness such as food poisoning and diarrhoea. Some people are also allergic to cockroaches and may get asthma. Treatments for these insects can be complex and cannot be resolved with two or three treatments. It is strongly advised that contact should be made to the council or another pest control company to carry out the work of eradication. Accurate survey work and assessments, plus a combination of monitoring traps and sprays or gel can eradicate roaches.

If you have an infestation of **Fleas**, make sure your pets are treated and use an effective insecticide for the home. Having had a flea treatment you shall see fleas emerging from the pupation – however, a residual insecticide will last for several weeks and gradually kill emerging fleas. Do not vacuum for at least three weeks after the treatment, and cover fish tanks during the treatment.

For **Ants**, the good news is you can definitively self-treat this annual pest. Use fresh insecticide powder if you have no pets or young children, or use a residual liquid/aerosol insecticide. Follow the ants back to the nest entrance, usually an area of high activity, and apply the insecticide according to the product instructions. It is very important to survey thoroughly for the nest site and to search beyond the outside of your house.

Preventing pests

It is better to prevent pests rather than waiting for them to arrive and then deal with the nuisance. Householders can assist in preventing infestations of pests by following a few simple measures, which are common to preventing numerous rodents and insects.

- Remove potential nesting sites by keeping gardens and yards clean and tidy and by cutting back overgrown areas.
- Do not feed wild birds or other animals to excess – you may be feeding rats, mice or pigeons as well.
- Keep your home in good repair so that pests cannot gain access into it. Mice can get into homes through gaps as small as 6mm.
- Insure that the drain inspection covers are in place and in good repair. Particularly look out for spaces under the doors, holes in the brickwork, and gaps around waste and water pipes.
- Do not leave household waste where pests can get access to it. Place all waste in a bin with a tight fitting lid.
- Do not dispose of waste food in your compost heap as it may attract rodents towards your property.
- Regularly clean up dog faeces and do not leave pet food or water bowls out during the night.
- A high standard of hygiene will deny sources of food and hiding places for insects.
- Food, especially sweet substances, should be kept out of the way with regards to ants.

Prevention is better than cure!

Household Tips

Diet and health tip

Skim off fat from soups and stews to keep fat content down.

If your drawers are sticking, rub along the edges with wax candles so that they run smoothly.

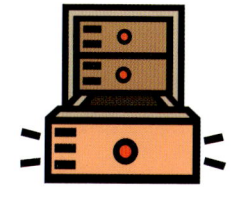

Added too much salt to a soup or stew? Add a couple of slices of potato to balance out the flavour.

Learn to switch off lights and appliances when not in use to cut down on electricity.

Freeze left over wine in bags or in ice cube trays to add to casseroles.

If you have an oil stain, sprinkle the stain with baby powder, leave for a day then rub the stain out.

Clean a dirty toilet bowl by pouring a can of coke down the toilet. Leave to soak then flush to remove all stains.

Danger Gas!

**Gas can be a very great friend or a deadly enemy.
If you smell gas, or suspect a gas leak:**

DO NOT smoke or strike matches
DO NOT turn electrical switches on or off

DO put out naked flames
DO open doors and windows
DO keep people away from the area affected
DO turn off the meter at the control valve

Safety : Your Number One Priority

Your gas should be checked regularly and a record of the safety check should be obtained and kept for two years. If you are a tenant, your landlord should have had all gas appliances and fittings checked for safety before letting the property to you, and you should receive a copy of the most recent gas safety check record. Also, all gas appliances should have ventilation and outlets. Landlords have a legal obligation to maintain all gas appliances in their properties, or they could be prosecuted.

Ask your landlord for information and copies of inspections, it's your life at stake!

Corgi

CORGI, or the 'Council for Registered Gas Installers', is the body charged with maintaining an accurate register of competent gas installers in Britain. It is a legal requirement for any business carrying out gas related work to be registered with CORGI.

Before allowing anyone to carry out gas related work on your property, either hired by yourself or your landlord, you should insist on seeing a CORGI ID card, which all registered installers are issued with.

To check the validity of the card presented, call 0870 401 2300 to speak to a CORGI customer services advisor who will check for you.

RELIGION

In this world there are 5 great religions. This is just a short resume of their beliefs. It may just give you an insight and help you cope with other people's beliefs and to try and understand the way that their religion affects their lives.

These snippets are in no way advocating a religion or belief. But merely to inform you and point out that there are no bad religions. Only that some of the people interpret the teachings differently to what the gods meant them to be.

BE GOOD. BE TOLERANT. THAT'S MY RELIGION.

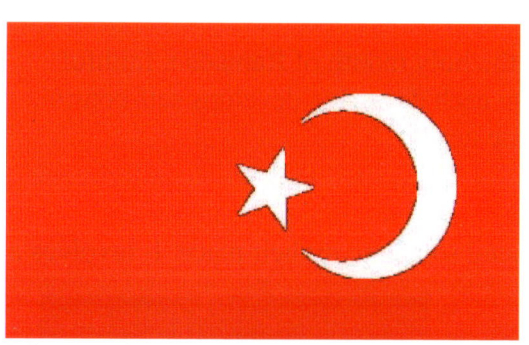

Basic Beliefs of Islam

The teachings of Islam are comprised of both faith and duty. There is no priesthood and no sacraments. The basis for Islamic doctrine is found in the Qur'an (Koran). It is the scripture of Islam, written by Muhammad and his disciples as dictated by the Angel Gabriel. It alone is infallible and without error.

Five Articles of Faith

The five articles of faith are the main doctrines of Islam. All Muslims are expected to believe the following:

1. **God.** There is one true God and his name is Allah.
2. **Angels.** Angels exist and interact with human lives.
3. **Scripture.** There are four inspired books, the Torah of Moses, the Psalms (Zabin) of David, the Gospel of Jesus Christ (Injil) and the Qur'an. Jews and Christians have corrupted all but the Qur'an.
4. **Prophets**. God has spoken through numerous prophets throughout time. The six greatest are: Adam, Noah, Abraham, Moses, Jesus and Muhammad. Muhammad is the last and greatest of all Allah's messengers.

5. **Last Days**. On the last day there will be a time of resurrection and judgement. Those who follow Allah and Muhammad will go to Islamic heaven, or paradise. Those who do not will go to hell.

The Five Pillars of Faith

1. Creed (Kalima)- One must state, 'There is no God but Allah, and Muhammad is the Prophet of Allah.'

2. Prayer (Salat)- Prayer must be done five times a day (upon rising, at noon, in mid-afternoon, after sunset, and before going to sleep) towards the direction of Mecca.

3. Almsgiving (Zakat)- Muslims are legally required to give one-fortieth of their income to the needy. Since those whom alms are given are helping the giver achieve salvation, there is no sense of shame in receiving charity.

4. Fastine (Ramadan)- During the holy month of Ramadan, faithful Muslims fast from sunup to sundown each day. This develops self-control, devotion to God, and identity with the needy.

5. Pilgrimage (Hajj)- Each Muslim is expected to make the pilgrimage to Mecca at least once in their lifetime is an essential part of gaining salvation, so the old or infirm may send someone in their place. It involves a set of rituals and ceremonies.

Basis Beliefs of Christianity

The central figure in Christianity is Jesus (or Christ), a Jew who came into this world by Immaculate Conception to a virgin named Mary. His birth is celebrated at Christmas with hymns and gift giving. This man was not only man, but also the Son of God and lived his life without sin.

During his lifetime, Jesus performed many miracles and spoke to many people about his father in heaven. He was arrested for claiming to be God's con and was hung on the cross by the Romans at age 33. Christians believe that the suffering and death upon the cross, which this sinless man endured, paid for the sins of all mankind, and because of Jesus' actions, salvation can be achieved by anyone who believes in him. This act of sacrifice is remembered during Lent.

Following his death, Christians believe that he rose from the grave (celebrated at Easter) and returned to the earth, appearing to his followers and telling them of the kingdom of God to which he was going. He also promised his disciples that he would return one day to bring all believers with him to that kingdom, to enjoy eternal life in the presence of God.

Christians can read of the life of Jesus, as well as his ancestors in the only Christian holy text, the Bible. It consists of the Old Testament and the New Testament.

Basic Beliefs of Hinduism

Hinduism is based on the concept that human and animal spirits reincarnate back to earth to live many times in different forms. The belief that souls move up and down an infinite hierarchy depending on the behaviors they practiced in their life is visible in many of the Hindu societal policies. The caste system survives and charity towards others is unheard of because each individual deserves to be in the social class they were born in. A person is born into poverty and shame because of misbehaviors in a past life.

Today, a Hindu can be polytheistic than one god), monotheistic (one god), paheistic (god and the universe are one), agnostic (unsure if god exists), or atheistic (no god) and still claim to be a Hindu.

The Hindu paths to salvation include the way of works (rituals), the way of knowledge (realization of reality and self-reflection), and the way of devotion (devotion to the god that you choose to follow). If the practitioner follows the paths of these ways, salvation can be achieved.

Basic Beliefs of Buddhism

The basic beliefs of Buddhism can be demonstrated in the following concepts and doctrines.

The Four Noble Truths

The First Noble Truth is the existence of suffering. Birth is painful and death is painful; disease and old age are painful. Not having what we desire is painful and having what we do not desire is also painful.

The Second Noble Truth is the cause of suffering. It is the craving desire for the pleasures of the senses, which seeks satisfaction now here, now there; the craving for happiness and prosperity in this life and in future lives.

The Third Noble Truth is the ending of suffering. To be free of suffering one must give up, get rid of, extinguish this very craving, so that no passion and no desire remain.

The Forth Noble Truth leads to the ending of all pain by way of the Eightfold Path.

The Eightfold Path

The First Step on that path is Right Views
The Second is Right Resolve
The Third is Right Speech
The Fourth is Right Behaviour
The Fifth is Right Occupation
The Sixth is Right Effort
The Seventh is Right Contemplation
The Eighth is Right Meditation

Buddhist Precepts

There are five precepts taught by Buddhism that all Buddhists should follow:
1. Kill no living thing
2. Do not steal
3. Do not commit adultery
4. Tell no lies
5. Do not drink intoxicants or take drugs

Basis Beliefs of Judaism

Judaism is a monotheistic religion, which believes that the world was created by a single, all knowing divinity, and that all things within that world were designed to have meaning and purpose as part of a divine order. According to the teachings of Judaism, God's will for human behaviour was revealed to Moses and the Israelites at Mount Saini. The Torah, or commandments, which regulate how humans are to live their lives, were a gift from God so that they might live in according to His will.

Statement of Faith

Moses Maimonides, a Spanish Jew who lived in the 12th century, tried to condense the basic beliefs of Judaism into the form of a creed. It is still followed by the traditional forms of Judaism.

Three Branches of Judaism

These are the three branches of Judaism which form the framework for the type of lifestyle and beliefs of Jewish individuals:

Orthodox-
> Traditionalists who observe most of the traditional dietary and ceremonial laws of Judaism

Conservative-
> Do not hold to the importance of a Jewish political state, but put more emphasis on the historic and religious aspects of Judaism, doctrinally somewhere between Orthodox and Reform

Reform-
> The liberal wing of Judaism, culture and race orientated with little consensus on doctrinal or religious belief

EMPLOYMENT AGENCIES\RECRUITMENT AGENCIES & TEMPING AGENCIES

Employers to fill jobs use these agencies. You register with these agencies (give them details of school\college\university qualifications or work you have done before and your contact details etc) and they will contact you with any jobs that come in from employers that they think are suitable for you.

Some agencies can even assist you in writing your Curriculum Vitae, which is a letter explaining what qualifications\work experience you have and can include goals\objectives\hobbies and interests that you may have. A C.V. is often vital as an introduction to a potential employer.

These agencies are listed in your local yellow pages, so if you are seeking a job it could be a good idea to register with as many agencies as possible. Don't just sit back and wait for the offers of work to roll in though, it is still important to get out there yourself and apply on your own.

Agencies can regularly go through periods where little or no work is available or your particular skills might not match the types of jobs coming in.

Get up and do it – only you can make it happen!

Signing On

Job Seekers Allowance / The Dole

This is for people who are out of work. Money is taken from tax and given in weekly amounts to people who are 'seeking' jobs but are unemployed. If you are out of work and struggling to get by applying for this could be a good idea. However it is not there to be relied upon, that is why every week you will have to make phone calls to your local job-centre to apply for jobs advertised at the centre. After six months if you have not got a job you will have to attend training that teaches you how to get a job in order to receive Job Seekers Allowance. This training can be quite humiliating but you will have to attend it if you want to receive your weekly allowance. Near the end of the training if you are under 21 the Job Centre may suggest that you return to education and even pay you an allowance to do so. Alternatively they may put you on 'New Deal'. This is for people who have had a long period of being unsuccessful at getting a job. Employers are actually paid to employ people that are on New Deal so it should be easier for New Deal candidates to get employment as it is in the interest of the employer. Failing all this you will be cut off and not allowed to reapply for any more allowance for six months. It is illegal to claim job seekers allowance if you are employed by anyone unless you are earning less than 16 hours a week. It is also illegal to be paid cash in hand with no record of the payment. Check if your employer is doing this as it could be you that is fined for breaking the law not just your employer if they are found out.

If you are eligible for Job Seekers Allowance you will need to go into your local job centre and give them some information about yourself and your circumstances.

Making a Will

It is important for you to make a will whether or not you consider you have many possessions or much money. It is important to make a will because if you die without one, there are certain rules which dictate how the money, property or possessions should be allocated, and it is unlikely that it be will be the same as the way you would have liked. Other reasons you should make a will are to ensure care of any children you may have after your death, to allow unmarried partners or partners who have not registered a civil partnership to inherit, or, following a change of circumstance, to ensure your money and possessions are distributed as you wish, for example after a separation.

If you are in any doubt as to whether or not you should make a will, you should consult a solicitor or a Citizens Advice Bureau, who will be able to provide you with a list of solicitors.

How to write a Will that is Valid

In order for a will to be valid, it must be:-

- made by a person who is 18 years old or over
- made voluntarily and without pressure from any other person
- made by a person who is of sound mind. This means the person must be fully aware of the nature of the document being written or signed and aware of the property and the identify of the people who may inherit
- in writing
- signed by the person making the will in the presence of two witnesses
- signed by those two witnesses, in the presence of the person making the will, after it has been signed. (A witness or the married partner of a witness cannot benefit from a will).

It is also advisable to ensure that the will includes the date on which it is signed. Once the will meets all of the above requirements and has been signed and witnessed, it is complete and legally valid.

Using a solicitor

There is no legal need for a will to be drawn up or witnessed by a solicitor, so you can write your will yourself if you want to. However, as it is easy to make mistakes in a will, it is often advisable to use a solicitor, or at least ask a solicitor to check the will over to ensure it will have the effect you intended. However, there will be a fee.

Football league teams

Fill each space with the name of a football team to retell the story in full.

The sun shone ………………………….. the ………………..………. morning as we set sail for the ……………………………. .
In a ship with a large green …………… ……..……As we sail down the river which ………………… ….. to the sea, we wave to a fair maiden leaning against the …………………………… .
　　The ……………….... was made up of Scots, Irish and others of the ………………… race. The exception was the cabin boy named ……………………. whose job it was to ……………..……. the boilers. He was illiterate though won our ……………..……. with his ……………..…… efforts to improve his …………… He was sent to …………………..by the other villains who had brought their…………………..of weapons on board. They were a rowdy bunch and after drinking they did in fact ……………………..furniture.
　　The voyage made my……………..……..as she had not had a holiday……………………..too long and the sea…………………….did her………………..lot of good. We landed……………….…...in the day on the…………………….of the island where the natives ……………….…….their dead. We crossed a……………………..and entered a dense………………...where the………………...roamed freely. We………………...regardless and

211

eventually met a group of……………..………dressed in……………..……green.
    After a days journey we caught dark fish in a………..…………and tried unsuccessfully to get milk from a herd of cows but they did not like having their…………..………At last we reached our destination, the house of Hawaii's monarch, the …..………..………She greeted us with a friendly……….…….but was very upset as her……….………had been smashed. She had no alternative but to live in a…………..………while she had a………..………built.
    When we found the treasure, we put the……….………the ship which we later sold investing half the proceeds in the………………..and the other half in the alliance and…………..……..We arrived home that night and had…………..……..cake and……….………buns followed by……………..…..which made us all ill.

You can see into the light from the dark,
but you can't see into the dark from the light.

If you want to find a fool in Ireland take one with you.

JML and Da.

Keep Your Brain Active
Tax Yourself Weekly With Simple Puzzles Like This:

Puzzle Page

1. **What is it?**
He who makes it doesn't want it.
He who buys it doesn't need it.
He who needs it doesn't know

2. **What Food Item do you:**
Throw away the outside,
Then cook the inside,
You then eat the outside,
Then throw away the inside.

3. What is the longest word in the English language?

4. How many cubic meters of dirt are in a hole 6 metres long, 2 metres wide, and one metre deep?

5. Which year did Christmas day and new years day fall in the same year.

6. Before Mount Everest was discovered, what was the highest mountain on earth?

7. The six letters in the word chesty can only be made into one other word, what is it?

8. From what number can you take away half and leave nothing?

9. What two questions can never be answered with a yes?

10. What five letter word does every Oxford graduate pronounce wrong?

11. Which is the only non English club to win the F.A.Cup?

12. When Clara Clatter was purchasing her new parrot, the salesman assured her that it would repeat any word it heard. About a week later, Clara returned the parrot complaining it hadn't uttered a single word. Given that the salesman had spoken the truth about the parrot's abilities, why wouldn't the bird talk?

13. Can you take away one letter from a six-letter word and leave twelve?

14. What word has three syllables and yet has 26 letters?

15. What costs two pounds for eight, four pounds for sixty-four and six pounds for five hundred and twelve?

16. How many of each species did Moses take onto the ark with him?

17. What happens twice in a moment, once every minute, but never in a hundred years?

18. Is it legal in Britain for a man to marry his widow's sister?

19. What five letter word becomes shorter when you add two letters to it?

20. How would you rearrange the letters in the words 'new door' to make one word? Note: There is only one correct answer.

21. I have in my hands two coins totalling 15p. One is not a 5p piece. Please remember that. What are they?

22. Two grandmasters played five games of chess. Each won the same number of games and lost the same number of games. There were no draws in any of the games. How could this be so?

23. You are pilot of an aeroplane with 100 passengers which drops of half in Birmingham and picks up 10, flies to Manchester, doubles its load and then finally reduces it by a third at Edinburgh. What is the pilot's name?

24. A woman had two sons who were born in the same hour of the same day in the same year, but they were not twins. How could this be so?

25. Why are 1988 pennies worth more than 1983 pennies?

26. What is it that gets wetter as it dries?

---

27. There were two Americans waiting at the entrance to the British Museum. One of them was the father of the other one's son. How could this be so?

Answers to Football league teams:

The sun shone Brighton the Wednesday morning as we set sail for the Orient in a ship with a large green Hull. As we sail down the river which Leeds to the sea, we wave to a fair maiden leaning against the Millwall.

    The Crewe was made up of Scots, Irish and others of the Celtic race. The exception was the cabin boy named Clyde whose job it was to Stoke the boilers. He was illiterate though won our Hearts with his Stirling efforts to improve his Reading He was sent to Coventry by the other villains who had brought their Arsenal of weapons on board. They were a rowdy bunch and after drinking they did infact Wrexham furniture.

    The voyage made my Motherwell as she had not had a holiday Forfar too long and the sea Ayr did her Chester lot of good. We landed Leighton in the day on the Southend of the island where the natives Bury their dead. We crossed a Mansfield and entered a dense Forest where the Wolves roamed freely. We Preston regardless and eventually met a group of Rangers dressed in Lincoln green.

    After a days journey we caught dark fish in a Blackpool and tried unsuccessfully to get milk from a herd of cows but they did not like having their Huddersfield At last we reached our destination, the house of Hawaiis monarch, the Queen of the South. She greeted us with a friendly Alloa but was very upset as her Crystal Palace had been smashed. She had no alternative but to live in a Villa while she had a Newcastle built.

    When we found the treasure, we put the Luton the ship which we later sold investing half the proceeds in the Halifax and the other half in the alliance and Leicester. We arrived home that night and had Dundee cake and Chelsea buns followed by Oldham which made us all ill.

Puzzle Solutions:

1. A Coffin
2. Corn on the Cob
3. Smiles (mile between the two s's!)
4. No dirt in hole
5. Every year
6. Mount Everest
7. Scythe
8. 8
9. Are you dead? Are you dumb?
10. Wrong
11. Cardiff
12. Parrot is dumb deaf
13. Dozens
14. Alphabet
15. Door numbers
16. Moses didn't?
17. The letter M
18. The man would be dead
19. Short
20. new door?
21. 10p and 5p (the other one is 5p)
22. They were playing different people
23. Your name
24. Triplets
25. One thousand nine hundred and eighty eight is more than one thousand nine hundred and eighty three
26. A mop
27. The other one is the mother

Acknowledgements

David Hill

Anthony Michael Slater
For his expertise on Tenancy Law

Harry (Henri) Mountain
Whose encouragement kept me going

John Holford

John Harvey

Heidi Baldwin

Johnnie Mountain

Carnmor Print

With special thanks to:
Sharon Roberts
For coming to my aid and pulling all the pieces together.
Without her, this book would remain unfinished.

Copyright © 2007 Tony Slater
The right of Tony Slater to be identified as the Author of the Work has been asserted by him in accordance with the Copyright, Designs and Patents act 1988.
First published in 2007, Sun-Fly Printing, China.
Every effort has been made to fulfil requirements with regard to reproducing copyright material. The author and publisher will be glad to rectify any omissions at the earliest opportunity